ICEFISHING
East and West

ICEFISHING
East and West

Jim Zumbo

Drawings by Jeff Johnson

David McKay Company, Inc.
New York

This book is dedicated to the memory of Lou Gizzarelli, my closest friend and fishing buddy, who despite a busy schedule, always had time to introduce youngsters to the world of the outdoors.

Library of Congress Cataloging in Publication Data

Zumbo, Jim.
Icefishing, East and West.

Includes index.
1. Ice fishing. I. Title.
SH455.45.Z85 799.1'2 78-10715
ISBN 0-679-51103-2

10 9 8 7 6 5 4 3 2 1

Manufactured in the United States of America

Acknowledgments

This book would never have been completed if it hadn't been for the assistance of many people. I'm grateful to a number of state agencies for providing information and photos, especially the Colorado Division of Wildlife Resources, Michigan Travel Commission, Minnesota Department of Economic Development, Minnesota Department of Natural Resources, Ohio Division of Wildlife, Pennsylvania Fish Commission, Utah Division of Wildlife Resources, and the Wisconsin Department of Natural Resources. More thanks go to Arctic Cat Enterprises Inc., Billy Boy Enterprises, The Coleman Company, Dickey Tackle Co., Houghton Lake Chamber of Commerce, L.L. Bean Inc., Normark Corp., Sheldon's Inc., and The Worth Company. And finally a personal thanks to these individuals, Merritt Benson, Parker N. Davies, M.D., Robert Demetry, Jerry Gibbs, Bob Gilsvik, Dennis Haberkorn, Wayne Nicolls, David Richey, and especially my lovely wife, Lois, who typed this book and provided guidance and moral support when the deadline drew near.

Contents

Introduction

Icefishing! The very word creates visions of mentally deranged persons giving way to masochistic tendencies by slowly freezing to death on top of a frozen lake. A closer look, however, reveals normal individuals who enjoy the productive activities of catching fish through a hole in the ice.

Modern technology has evolved icefishing paraphernalia to the point where comfort on the ice is the rule rather than the exception. Today, female family members are as much a part of the icefishing scene as their male counterparts. Kids are great fans, too.

Why do people shun the warm confines of a comfortable home to expose themselves to fickle winter weather? For openers, icefishing is productive—make no mistake about it. As you'll read elsewhere in this book, ice anglers are usually more successful than open-water fishermen. Icefishing is a gregarious sport. Fishermen are a sociable lot, and angling through the ice lends itself to good companionship and plain old fun, whether you're fishing for rainbow trout on a Wyoming lake or for yellow perch in a Michigan shanty town.

Ice angling is not a recent sport, but it grows bigger and better every year. Shanty towns spring up on lakes every winter throughout the Lake States, Midwest, and Northeast. Whole communities move onto the ice for their favorite sport, and local contests and celebrations make this a festive time of the year. In the West, icefishing continues to become more popular as swelling ranks of westerners learn to catch trout and panfish through the lid of a frozen lake.

Icefishing depends on cold temperatures, so it is possible only in the northern portions of North America. The states of Michigan, Wisconsin, and Minnesota are the "Big 3" leaders in the sport, followed closely by Ohio, Pennsylvania, Illinois, New York, New Jersey, Iowa, Nebraska, Indiana, the Dakotas, and all New England states.

Temperate states like Tennessee, Kentucky, Oklahoma, Delaware, and Missouri might freeze their ponds and lakes in any given year. When they do, enthusiastic groups of anglers converge and ply their wares as long as the ice holds.

More lakes and reservoirs are appearing in the arid West, so more Western anglers are following the ice on high-elevation lakes. Even fishermen in dry states such as Utah, Arizona, and New Mexico have an assortment of ponds and impoundments in which to fish through the ice.

Like every outdoor sport, icefishing has its own unique thrills. The magic words "Flag-up," send millions of tip-up fishermen scurrying madly across the ice of thousands of lakes each winter season. When the spring thaws finally arrive and claim the beloved ice, the ice angler stores his tackle for another year. Forgotten are the frostbitten fingers, the bitter winds, the dull, stubborn auger, and the numb toes. The season was a success as long as the bobber occasionally zipped below the ice hole and the tip-up flag fluttered its merry signal to all who could see.

Icefishermen suffer from illusions, and are probably a little schizophrenic. Their brains tell them they're enjoying themselves while their bodies might be on the brink of hypothermia. They talk to fellow ice anglers who they would avoid in summer. They offer gifts of hot tea, coffee, chocolate, and perhaps home brew to strangers who are catching fish, hoping that they can learn their secrets. They grudgingly sacrifice their chores around the house so they can bring home a half-dozen fish for the family freezer. They even forsake weekend football games, and maybe church services, so that they can provide valuable nutritional fish for their children. They claim that icefishing has therapeutic values that can't be found elsewhere—after all, don't the local doctor and veterinarian icefish every Sunday?

This book is written for those wonderful folk who like to spend their time fishing through the top of a frozen lake. The chapters will explore time-honored habits and procedures, and will present modern changes that continually update the sport.

The fun part about writing this book was the excuse it gave me to spend a disproportionate amount of my time on the ice. Friendships were made, secrets were revealed, and even a few fish were caught. Above all, every hour on the ice was spent in doing what I enjoyed most—forgetting the problems of the civilized world and having fun. What else could top that?—*J.Z.*

All About Ice and the Water Beneath It

Basics About Ice

Ice! Few substances are as demanded, unwanted, cussed, and discussed as much as ice. Found naturally throughout much of the world, at both poles and at very high elevations ice is often perennial. In other regions, it is artificially manufactured in millions of refrigerators and freezers.

On the minus side, ice clogs our rivers and carburetors, coats our highways and sidewalks, jams our car doors and rain gutters, and breaks our trees and branches. We scrape it, sand it, salt it, slip on it, and swear at it.

On the plus side, it is used to cool our food, soothe our bruises, and freshen our drinks. We chop it, chip it, crush it, and crack it.

And we fish through it. Wherever there is ice on a lake or river, there will be ice fishermen.

Most of us never think twice about how ice forms. We take the process for granted: when air turns cold enough, the lake freezes. A closer look, however, reveals a systematic series of events that occurs year after year.

In order to understand the phenomenon, let's look at a cross section of a lake. There are three characteristic layers of water in a typical, deep, northern lake during the summer and early fall. These layers, or strata, are known as the epilimnion, the thermocline, and the hypolimnion.

The epilimnion is a layer of warm water that is affected by wind action and whose temperatures closely follow changes and trends in air temperatures. This layer is the uppermost stratum of a lake, and its thickness is influenced by wind, temperature, physical characteristics of the lake, latitude, and local climatic conditions.

The thermocline is the middle layer, and it's temperatures decrease more rapidly than those in either of the other layers.

The bottom layer, the hypolimnion, is the area where the water is coldest in the summer and early fall. Oxygen is often depleted in this layer, and the water temperature seldom exceeds 45° F.

As fall progresses and the water in the epilimnion layer starts to cool, the water contracts and becomes heavier. This heavy water sinks to the bottom and displaces warmer, lighter water, which rises to the top. This process, called turnover, continues until the water temperature throughout the lake reaches a uniform temperature of about 39° F.

As the air temperature continues to drop, so does the temperature of the surface water of the lake. When the surface water reaches 32° F., ice begins to form along the shoreline. If the air remains calm and the temperature stays cold enough, ice strengthens and builds until the entire surface of the lake is glazed. Continued cold aids the freezing process, and the ice continues to thicken. Alternating snows, rains, thaws, and freezes contribute to the ice thickness from the top and forms "snow-ice."

The ultimate ice thickness depends on the extremes of air temperature through the winter season. In Canada and some of our northern states, 36 to 40 inches of ice is common. In Maryland and West Virginia, however, 2 to 4 inches might be the maximum. Ice thickens quickest at the very beginning of cold weather. Most of the ice forms within the first four weeks of winter in areas where very cold air persists. As more water freezes along the underside of the ice, the thickening layer becomes a better and better insulator and, thus, slows down the formation of additional ice. This is true even when temperatures drop well below zero. Constant snow cover adds yet another blanket of insulation to the ice.

Large, deep lakes are slower to freeze than smaller bodies of water. It takes longer for the "turnover" process to be completed, and wind action prevents the formation of new ice. Bear Lake, which straddles the Utah–Idaho border is over 100 feet deep in places. It receives substantial winter winds which keep the surface constantly churned. It seldom freezes before February even though temperatures commonly plunge to—20° F. When it does freeze, four to eight inches is about the normal thickness since the freezing process occurs so late in the year.

In contrast, consider Lake Champlain on the New York–Vermont border. Ice forms early on this big lake; by February there is up to 30 inches of ice.

Some large lakes have sheltering bays or coves that are relatively calm, and they never freeze entirely, although many of the protected coves can be counted on to ice over each year. Famous Flaming Gorge Reservoir on the Utah–Wyoming border is an example.

Other lakes never freeze because of springs that contribute warm water to the lake bottom. This is especially true in shallow lakes. In deeper lakes, ice often forms over the spring area, but it may remain thin and weak, forming a treacherous zone that should never be traveled on.

Creeks, streams, and rivers often carry warm water into lakes, and ice in the vicinity of these inlets is also weak. Since these areas are often good places to find fish, the cautious angler should approach them with care and cut holes where the ice is safe. No fish is worth the risk of breaking through weak ice.

An important physical law involving water has a profound influence on the way our lakes freeze. It declares that fresh water is at maximum density at a temperature of 39.2° F. At temperatures above or below this point, water becomes lighter and rises. The fact that water becomes heaviest at 39.2° F. and sinks means that lakes freeze from the top to the bottom. Obviously, if the water froze from the bottom up, lakes in temperate and colder regions would freeze solidly and might never melt completely in the summer. Imagine what that would do to our fishing—and to our lives!

Knowledge of water temperatures under ice helps us understand why fish react the way they do. It explains why some fish spend the winter in the warmest water at the bottom of the lake, and why others are found at different levels, even directly under the ice. Since fish are cold-blooded creatures, their body temperature adjusts to the temperature of the water surrounding them. In an ice-covered lake, the water temperature is between 32° F. and 39.2° F. Despite this small range fish are acutely aware of even a one degree change and will be attracted to areas where they are most comfortable.

Warm-water species such as walleyes and yellow perch hug the bottom of the lake where the water is warmest. But how about the lake trout, a fish that is known to thrive in the coldest and deepest part of the lake? These large trout prefer the bottom area, too, despite the fact that they're more adapted to colder waters near the ice layer above. Food availability may account for this apparent contradiction.

It should be obvious that a lake, even one locked under a mantle of thick ice, is a dynamic entity that yields no easy conclusions based on logic alone. Dozens of interrelated factors determine where, why, and how the fish behave the way they do. Only experience can unlock the secrets, and, even then, we can only scratch the surface.

Fish are unpredictable under the ice, but we can learn enough about them to catch them with far greater consistency than if we were totally ignorant about their behavioral patterns.

After all, if we could figure why fish bite best on some days and not on others, or why fish bite better during certain hours of the day, then icefishing would lose much of its challenge and charm. Who wants to see icefishing degenerate into a ho-hum, blasé sport where there are no little secrets and contradictions?

Ice-Out

So far this chapter has discussed the formation of ice. What happens in spring, when ice gives way to longer, warmer days? Let's take a look.

Ice begins to melt with the very first signs of spring. Extra daylight hours and increased air temperatures trigger subtle changes in the ice layer. A good share of the melting process takes place unobserved on the underside of the ice as the sun's heat is conducted through the ice to the water below. Since the undersurface is in contact with this warmed water, it melts much faster than the top of the ice that is in contact with warm surface air.

Air temperature is the most important factor that determines the speed and extent of ice deterioration. Sunshine accelerates the rate of melting in cooperation with warm air temperatures. It stands to reason that small lakes, with their thicker ice and greater protection from winds, will open later than larger ones. High altitude lakes will retain their ice cover longer than lower lying waters. Tidal rivers usually open quickly because of the constant currents under the ice. In addition, these rivers seldom have thick ice because of moving surface water and high salinity rates.

When ice nears the final stages of breakup, it turns watery and honeycombed and, often, gives the impression of being black. At this point, a good wind and warm rain will be all that's necessary to allow the lake to triumph over the substance that sealed it all winter.

Ice in this condition is completely unsafe, yet overzealous anglers occasionally take foolish chances for "one last shot of the season." I've seen fishermen throw planks out in front of them to reach a spot thirty yards from shore when ice was honeycombed. If ice is so unpredictable that boards are needed to assist travel, the only advice is to stay off. If you *must* fish, find another pond that has thicker ice. Better yet, gather your gear and pack it away for next winter.

Lake Classification

This chapter wouldn't be complete if it didn't address the classification of lakes. Lake type may explain fish behavior under the ice, so it's important to have a basic understanding of the kind of water we're fishing.

There are two basic types of lakes: oligotrophic and eutrophic. The former lake is characterized by clear, deep waters, with little food and nourishment. The latter lake is more productive, with adequate foods and plants.

Oligotrophic lakes have little decaying organic matter in the deeper areas, but have a cold, well-oxygenated hypolimnion. These lakes have excellent habitats for lake trout. They are young geologically, and will mature as nutrients increase and basins begin to fill in.

Eutrophic lakes are home to warm-water fish rather than trout, since oxygen may be depleted to the point where levels are lethal to trout. In these lakes, the process of decomposition may lower oxygen levels to the point where there is winterkill.

A few lakes are classified as dystrophic. This is a body of water that is essentially stagnant due to decaying vegetation. The water is usually brown and acidic because of the sphagnum mosses and other types of vegetation that discolor it. Some Adirondack and Canadian lakes fall into this category.

It's interesting to note that all lakes are ephemeral: they're temporary bodies of water. Many waters in the United States have already disappeared and are now totally filled and covered with woodlands. Modern man isn't helping the situation. We're hastening the extinction of lakes by adding sewage and fertilizer to our natural water systems. Fortunately, restrictions on phosphates and other forms of nutrients are helping to slow down the filling in of lakes.

Oxygen and Temperature —The Secret to Fishing Success

Oxygen—a Most Critical Factor

Fish require oxygen for survival. Since they live in water, the oxygen they use is in dissolved form. Sometimes there is adequate oxygen, and sometimes there isn't. Since fish are captives in a lake, they are literally victims of their environment. Although fish can and do seek out levels and areas where oxygen is adequate, in some situations no such havens exist.

Oxygen supply is vital during winter, when a lake is sealed off from the atmosphere by a layer of ice. Anglers who recognize this fact seek areas where oxygen levels, combined with low water temperatures, cause fish to behave differently than they do in open water situations.

In order to learn how fish react to oxygen supply, it's necessary to understand the oxygen cycle in a typical lake. Oxygen enters a body of water in three distinct ways: through photosynthesis, via feeder streams, creeks, and springs, and from the atmosphere.

Plants—Important Oxygen Factories

Photosynthesis is a process that plants use to produce oxygen. By taking in carbon dioxide and water, plants manufacture simple sugar and give off oxygen as a by-product. Since sunlight is critical to the oxygen-making process, photosynthesis obviously occurs only in lighted portions of a lake or river.

When ice and snow cover a body of water and shut out the light, plants are unable to produce oxygen. In most lakes covered by ice, a reverse process commonly occurs. Plants that can't produce oxygen will die. As they decay and decompose, they use valuable amounts of oxygen in the process. Wholesale depletion of oxygen can occur when great quantities of vegetation decompose at the same time. So the plants, which once breathed life into the thriving lake, now rob the very waters that they once nourished.

If oxygen depletion is severe, fish that can't tolerate low oxygen levels will die first. The term for this type of mortality is winterkill. Fish that are exposed to this critical shortage of oxygen actually suffocate, much the same as we would if our oxygen supply were eliminated.

The amount of oxygen dissolved in the water is expressed as parts per million (p.p.m.). Trout normally require 10 p.p.m. (that is—10 parts of oxygen for 1 million parts of water), while most warm-water species need only 5 parts per million. Oxygen is so critical that the loss of 1 part per million in a lake may be lethal to fish.

Let's say a particular lake that supported a wide variety of fish suffered severe winterkill. If the oxygen level fell below 10 parts per million, the first fish to die would be the trout. As the oxygen continued to be depleted, bass, bluegills, and yellow perch would succumb next. As the oxygen level continued downward, carp and catfish would suffocate, leaving a barren lake with no fish life whatsoever.

What does all this have to do with catching fish through the ice? First of all, fish may stop feeding if they're distressed because of oxygen depletion. This behavior might be common in shallow ponds and might explain why fish refuse to bite in certain waters during the winter.

I know a small lake in the West where huge bluegills bite furiously in spring and summer. It's another story during winter, however. Despite the large bluegill population, the fish absolutely refuse to bite in the winter. It's my theory that the fish are distressed because of low oxygen levels in the winter and simply do not feed. The late has an incredible amount of underwater vegetation in the summer. Since the ice layer becomes very thick in the winter and clouds over because of snow, little sunlight penetrates through the ice. Much vegetation dies and feeds on the lake's oxygen level as it decomposes. Each spring, hundreds and sometimes thousands of dead bluegills wash ashore. One year, I visited the lake a day after the ice had melted, and retrieved over 1,100 dead bluegills that lined the shore. They made a valuable contribution to my compost pile.

The loss of winterkilled bluegills in the lake doesn't seem to affect the fishing in the summer. In fact, biologists speculate that the annu-

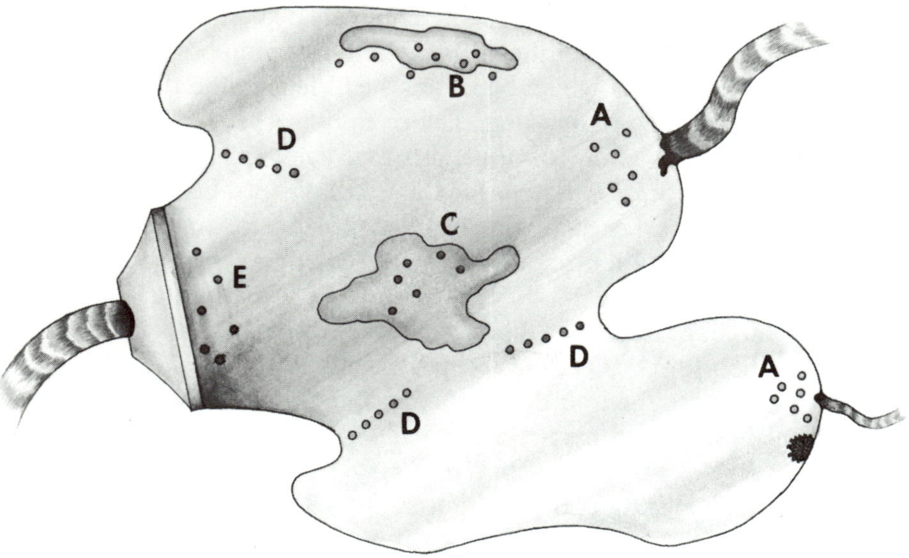

Some choice spots for jigging or for placing tip-ups. Warm-water fish may concentrate in these areas because of oxygen level, vegetation, or other physical factors. Areas marked "A" would appeal to most fish because of the influx of oxygenated waters from streams and creeks. Note the beaver lodge at the lower right adjacent to the small brook. Area marked "B" is shallow and weedy and would be a good spot for chain pickerel. Tip-ups should be set in and around weeds. Area "C" is a deep-water weedy area. It's a prime spot for northern pike. Tip-ups should be scattered through the weedy area. Areas marked "D" are promising for walleyes, since these fish are known to roam the shoreline. Walleyes should readily see tip-ups placed there. Area "E" near the dam is a good spot for yellow perch because the water is deep there.

al mortality rate is actually beneficial to the overall population because it keeps the fish community thinned and prevents stunting.

On larger lakes, it's possible to cash in on oxygen-rich areas by fishing along windswept shores where the wind keeps the ice free of snow. Since sunlight is allowed to penetrate the clear ice, underwater plants continue to grow and produce oxygen. Fish seek these areas and remain around them if oxygen levels are lethal elsewhere in the lake.

I tested this technique while fishing for pickerel on a Vermont lake. The ice was 22-inches thick and completely clouded. There was virtually no sunlight reaching the plants on the bottom—9 feet below the ice. Four hours of fishing produced 1 small pickerel. From time to time I picked strands of dead vegetation from my minnows as they swam just off the bottom.

The decaying vegetation bothered me since it indicated that there was inadequate oxygen below. Then I had an idea. A wind blew across the ice from the west, so I walked over to the exposed western shoreline and found that the ice was much clearer than where we had been fishing. It was obvious that constant winds kept the ice relatively snow-free. As an experiment, I cut a hole, tied on a spoon, and allowed it to plunge to the bottom. I intended to snag some underwater weeds to see what condition they were in. The spoon had hardly settled when my rod was almost jerked from my hands. A lively tussle produced a feisty pickerel almost two feet long.

I called my companions and held up the fish. It took no coaxing for them to walk over and cut holes near mine. Three hours later we had iced 11 pickerel, using the same technique that we had tried before.

It was interesting to note that the vegetation in that spot was green and growing. I concluded that the pickerel were attracted to that particular shoreline because of the clearer ice and higher oxygen level beneath it. The two areas were almost identical except for the condition of the plants and the ice.

An interesting study by a Michigan biologist showed how varying ice thicknesses and snow cover affected the transmission of light into the water below the ice layer. A 7 1/2 inch mantle of clear ice allowed about 85 percent of the light to pass through. Three inches of clear ice with just 1 inch of snow on top allowed only 10 percent of the light to penetrate. Five inches of snow over 3 inches of clear ice blocked out all but 1 to 3 percent of the light. Cloudy ice that was 15 inches thick stopped all but 10 to 12 percent of the light. In addition to these findings, he learned that clean, fresh snow allows the best transmission of light, followed by clean wet snow, and finally by granular snow. However, 5 inches of snow is enough to effectively shut down photosynthesis altogether. A certain degree of photosynthesis is possible when 10 to 12 percent of the light penetrates the ice and reaches the vegetation below.

Oxygen Via Streams and Springs

The second manner in which oxygen enters a lake is via a stream, creek, or spring. Dissolved oxygen is usually plentiful in streams because of the constant turbulence which exposes the water to the air. Streams are therefore oxygen-rich waters that recharge lakes at the inlet area where they enter.

During periods of oxygen deficiency, fish may linger around inlets because of the obvious abundance of oxygen. Although inlets may be a productive place to fish, care should be taken in the vicinity because of the danger of thin ice. The constant flow of water on the underside of the ice layer tends to hinder ice from thickening.

Most streams and creeks entering a lake are visible, but others are not, especially those along a marshy shoreline. A tiny brook can enter a lake unnoticed, particularly if there is a little open water to give it away.

Several years ago I discovered a simple way to locate oxygen-rich feeder creeks. I was trapping beaver at the time and had made a number of sets around a lodge at the edge of a frozen lake. The beaver lodge was the typical high mound, and it was located just adjacent to a small brook that discretely entered the lake. There was enough open water where the brook entered the lake for the beaver to swim from the lodge directly to the running water, and then up to the shore where fresh food could be obtained.

As I trapped in other lakes, I noticed that enough beaver lodges were located close to tiny brooks so as not to be coincidental. It was logical that the mammals (which are active all winter) should construct their living quarters in proximity to open water. Beavers are usually sealed in their lodges for the duration of the winter and are forced to eat twigs and branches from an under-ice food cache that they gathered in the fall. Animals that can find a way above the ice can eat fresh bark and twigs rather than the slime-covered, waterlogged material in their underwater food caches.

Even though I recognized that beaver lodges were apt to be near a small inlet, I didn't appreciate the fact that fish in an ice-bound lake would be attracted there. One day I approached a lodge near a brook and was amazed to see literally thousands of shiners and dace milling around the mouth of the creek. It was obvious that they were distressed because many of them gasped for air at the surface. The next day I cut several holes around the inlet and jigged for yellow perch. Almost immediately I found fish, and in two hours I had all I could carry. It was apparent that perch were enjoying the oxygenated waters since the other parts of the lake yielded few fish. Stomach analysis of several perch discounted the possibility that the minnows attracted them since their bellies were empty. Oxygen seemed to be the key attraction.

Springs that enter lakes underwater seldom contribute much oxygen, since their waters originate and travel underground, where oxygen is minimal. However, a little oxygen is better than none, so fish often congregate around them. Underwater springs may also attract fish because their water is warmer than that of the lake. As in the case of stream inlets, caution is always advised around spring areas since warm discharge water reduces ice thickness.

It's difficult to find springs that enter a lake from an underground source. Thin ice is an indicator, but can't always be counted on. Many times ice will cloud over because of snow, and no differences in thickness can be determined.

Springs can be located during open water periods by using a thermometer. Cool readings in a localized area generally indicate the presence of a spring. Vegetative growth is often different near a spring, and may be heavier and denser where cool water flows in. By marking springs on a map or committing their locations to memory, the ice angler can cut his holes near these productive areas. I like to record spring locations by triangulating with shoreline objects. I carry a small pad and draw the locations so I won't forget several months later. That way there's little guesswork and I can pinpoint my holes with accuracy.

Atmospheric Oxygen

The last way that oxygen enters a lake is through contact of the surface water with the atmosphere. Turbulent waters, caused by wind, speed up oxygen exchange. Breaking whitecaps and waves dashing against the shoreline enable more oxygen to enter the water. Of course, a lake sealed by ice has no chance to be enriched by atmospheric oxygen. Some lakes, however, never freeze over completely because of constant wind action. Generally speaking, those lakes are usually very deep. Although they may not freeze over entirely, protected bays and coves often develop a thick layer of ice. More often than not, these spots are quite productive. Flaming Gorge, as mentioned in the previous chapter, is a good example of a deep lake that doesn't freeze. During most years, however, the bays and protected flats are covered with thick ice. In this impoundment and others like it, trout never suffer from a lack of oxygen.

Temperature

As mentioned briefly in the previous chapter, fish are classified as cold-blooded animals. Basically, this means that their body temperature will equal that of the outside environment. A fish swimming in 35° water, for example, will have a body temperature of about 35°. When the water temperature increases to 75°, the fish's body temperature will also be the same.

This characteristic explains why fish act differently in the winter and summer. When water temperature drops to low levels, fish behavior changes dramatically. They become somewhat lethargic and don't require as much food as they do when the water is warmer. Fish go on a maintenance diet under the ice and eat only enough to sustain their body weight. In fact, they're known to lose weight in the winter.

This slowing down of body metabolism explains why biologists can determine the age of fish by counting the rings on their scales, much like the technique used to ascertain the age of a tree. When fish grow slowly in the winter, the scales grow slowly too. Cells are closer together, giving a compressed appearance. Under a microscope, the dense, small cells are distinct and form a dark ring.

George Teaches Me About Temperature

A pet bass taught me much about fish behavior in relation to changes of water temperature. I rescued George from a small brook that was about to dry up in the middle of a New York summer. As soon as George adapted to my aquarium, he soon eliminated every other living thing in his new home. A number of crayfish, bluegills, shiners, and dace were quickly consumed by the hungry fingerling bass.

A heater in the aquarium kept the temperature at a constant 70° F. In this environment, George ate from three to six minnows every other day. He kept this rate up for several months and had grown from three inches to nine inches by the time winter set in.

Since the aquarium was located in a fruit storage room that got quite cold, I decided to experiment and vary the water temperature. I turned off the heater, and in a day the water temperature decreased to 50°. George immediately stopped eating and allowed minnows to swim unmolested in the aquarium. As the days passed, I was able to determine that he ate only one minnow every three or four days. When I turned on the heater and warmed the water back to 70°, George quickly regained his voracious appetite. George reacted in typical fashion. With water at optimum temperature levels, he fed well and grew quickly. But with water temperatures low, his body had little food demand.

Though my experiments might imply that fish should bite poorly under the ice, this isn't the case. Icefishing is extremely productive.

Natural food is limited in winter, and a lure or bait dangling in the water may be the only food-like object the fish has seen for days. Fish are curious creatures and may strike just out of annoyance or merely to grab the lure before another fish does. Finally, fish need to eat something during winter, and your lure may be just the answer to their empty stomachs.

The fact that icefishing is productive doesn't mean the sport is a lead-pipe cinch. Plenty of work is often required to find fish, and a bit of innovation is necessary to entice them to strike.

The best way to find out for yourself is to get out there and try it. Don't be surprised if you find yourself learning something new every day you're on the ice!

How To Catch the Trouts

Trout—Cold-Water Fish

Trout are cold-water species and are quite at home under the ice. The extreme water temperature in a frozen lake doesn't slow down members of the trout family as much as it does warm-water species. Once, on a Western lake, I lay down on the ice, covered my head with a dark jacket, and peered into a hole. With the outside light cut off, I was able to see into the water. (The same effect is possible in darkened shanties.) A number of trout swam freely about, and I watched several move about in the vegetation that covered the bottom. They were highly active despite the very cold water. This makes them highly cooperative to the winter angler since active fish feed constantly.

This chapter will cover the "Big Four" members of the trout family: rainbows, brooks, browns, and lake trout. A fifth trout, the cutthroat, will be discussed along with rainbows since angling techniques for both are similar. Two other species, the Dolly Varden and Arctic Char, are taken in the West and in Canada, but interest in them is local. All trout display similar behavioral patterns under the ice, although each species has its own distinctive pecularities. The lake trout differs most from other trout.

Rainbows and Cutthroats

Rainbow trout (*Salmo gairdneri*) are the most universal of the North American trout. From a native habitat in the West, these fish have been introduced coast to coast, and as far south as they can survive. The rainbow owes its name to a broad band of red and pink that runs the length of each side. Small black spots pepper the fish

This Eastern angler looks at a pan-size trout he took on a tip-up. Trout are readily taken on tip-ups and on jigging rods. *Photo courtesy of Pennsylvania Fish Commission.*

from head to tail. An olive back rounds out the colors that mark this beautiful fish.

Rainbows possess no special mystique, yet they are revered by many. There is a certain amount of irony in this attitude because rainbows possess the most nondiscriminating taste buds of all the trout. Like coyotes and black bears, they'll eat practically anything that comes along, whether it moves or not.

Despite these eating habits, rainbows are not necessarily easy to catch. Whether you angle for them in open water or under the ice, a few basic rules apply everywhere.

One of my favorite rainbow lakes is on a Western Indian reservation. Ice anglers use every conceivable type of bait in this lake, including cheese, marshmallows, salmon eggs, spoons, jigs, and other assorted hardware. Baits have the edge over artificials, but the fish change their appetites almost daily. They might be hitting garlic cheese one day, but they'll be wanting marshmallows a day later.

One day I arrived late at the lake and found my companions in the usual area. I cut a hole in the midst of my buddies and dunked a glob of salmon eggs into the water. Up until that point, fishing had been slow, and my friends had caught only two trout in an hour. They were all using a marshmallow-cheese combination that was deadly the previous day.

My bait had hardly hit the bottom when a rainbow tugged rapidly. I set the hook and hauled a fat 15-incher onto the frozen lake. I rebaited, plopped the rig back into the water, and immediately tied into another. This pattern repeated itself until I had several rainbows flopping on the ice. Finally, my friends switched to salmon eggs. Action picked up at once, and we had all the fish we wanted in two hours.

Why the rainbows spurned the bait that was so successful the day before is anyone's guess. This is another example that illustrates the wisdom of being flexible. If a bait or lure works well one day, it might be a bummer the next. The wise angler switches baits and techniques until the right combination catches fish.

Rainbows move freely about under the ice and seldom remain stationary in one area as do other species, particularly warm-water fish. Thus, a large number of holes in a localized area may not be the answer to a luckless day. Instead, a move across the lake or to another bay or cove might be productive. If the lake has a marginal oxygen supply, a stream or river inlet may be the place to fish.

Another way to attract trout is to throw chum into the hole. Bits of cheese, crushed egg shells, corn, and oatmeal are also effective in getting a rainbow's attention. Be sure to check on the fishing regulations; some states prohibit using chum or corn.

One particular lake baffles me. Rainbows consistently run much larger along one shoreline than any of the others, yet all the areas exhibit the same physical characteristics, ice, and snow cover. It's tough to catch a trout less than two pounds in this spot, but smaller fish are the rule throughout the rest of the lake. For some reason, only the largest rainbows congregate in that particular location.

This shows the advantage of knowing a lake, regardless of the quarry. There is no question that some areas are definitely more productive than others. I wouldn't have known about this spot if I hadn't picked up a youngster who was hitchhiking next to the lake. The boy carried a crowbar, a standard spinning rod, and a heavy stringer of heavyweight rainbows. I had never seen fish that size come from the lake. In the course of conversation, he told me that he caught them on the far south shore, where there was no road access. A one-mile walk was required to get there, so he literally had the place to himself. Not for long, though. The following weekend the boy and I fished side-by-side, and scored easily on chunky, oversized trout.

The typical rainbow angler starts his day by fishing just off bottom. If no action is forthcoming, a change in depths might work. Sometimes, trout may reject baits altogether and savagely attack marabou jigs or hardware.

Whenever one angler seems to have all the success, there's usually a good reason. Is he using a lighter line that is more limber and invisible? Is his bait or lure different in a subtle way? Does he jig his lure with an imperceptible twitch? Find out what he's doing differently.

Rainbows are usually pursued with jigging rods, but anglers occasionally use tip-ups, where they are legal. I've taken rainbows in New York with tip-ups using garden worms for bait. Since rainbows don't usually engulf a bait and make off with it as do other fish, they don't normally lend themselves to tip-up fishing. Of course, lunker rainbows are a different story, but the pan-size variety pursued by the majority of today's ice fishermen are finicky biters. Small rainbows will often nibble at a bait and fail to trip the flag on the tip-up. If they do trigger the flag, odds are good that the fish won't be around by the time the angler races over to set the hook. In order for the flag to be tripped, the fish must make contact with the bait and move off with it. The turning reel has a small attachment that activates the flag and allows it to spring up.

Don't be afraid to pull out all the stops when fishing for rainbows. If one lure doesn't work, another might. If one area of a lake doesn't produce, try another location. Finally, don't be afraid to ask a successful fisherman what his secrets are. If he's a typical icefisherman, he'll tell you.

Cutthroat trout (*Salmo clarki*) are fish of the West. This trout displays two distinctive red slashes below the lower jaw which give it its name. Cutts, as they are often called by Western anglers, come

A chunky rainbow is hoisted above the ice of a Western lake by Danny Zumbo, son of the author. The trout took a cheese bait, one of the most popular baits in the West.

in many races and subspecies, many of them extremely rare. These fish have never been able to withstand heavy angling pressure, and don't compete well with other fish species. They also have a tendency to hybridize with rainbows when the two are in the same waters. Because of these limitations, care is taken to raise pure strain fish in hatcheries to keep the species uncontaminated. Despite this somewhat bleak appraisal, cutthroat trout are relatively abundant in many Western waters, and ice anglers pursue them along with other species. Many of the lakes they're found in are located at high elevations, and vehicle access may be impossible. Snowmobiles, cross-country skis, or snowshoes are often the only ways to get into cutthroat lakes.

The same lures and baits used for rainbows will work for cutts, although lures and marabou jigs are usually more effective. I know of one particular impoundment where two inch red and white spoons are deadly offerings.

Be sure to check carefully the laws of the state you intend to fish;

many high trout lakes may be closed to winter angling. Check to see if you have enough fishing line on your reel before pursuing rainbows and cutthroats. These fish are usually found in moderately deep water, often over 40 feet. A day's outing might be a failure if you were fishing an area 45 feet deep but had only 35 feet of line on your reel. Carry a well filled reel, as well as an extra spool of fresh, good quality line.

Brook Trout

Brook trout (*Salvelinus fontinalis*), like the rainbows, have been introduced all over North America. Brookies are as well established in Oregon as they are in Maine.

This fish, which is the smallest of American trout species, is also one of the most beautiful. It displays dark wavy lines on its back, with yellow spots and red spots surrounded by blue rings on the sides. The belly is often orange and black, and the fins are orange or reddish edged with black and white stripes. Since its tail is only slightly forked or not at all, it's commonly called a "squaretail."

Brook trout bite well under ice. So well, in fact, that some lakes may be closed to prevent an overharvest.

Brookies are capable of quickly overpopulating a lake and stunting. This is especially true if a lake has a low-fertility environment. When this occurs, increased harvest is often an acceptable tool in thinning populations to levels that are more in balance with the carrying capacity of the lake.

Brookies will hit a variety of lures and baits under the ice, but I've had my best luck using a silver Swedish Pimple sweetened with a mousee larvae. I fish with the lure about two feet off the bottom and jig it with a slow, sweeping motion. At times I've taken fish several feet off the bottom.

Like all trout, this fish has a high oxygen demand. Stream inlets and areas of clear ice may be more productive than other locations. In one northeast lake, I had consistent success by cutting holes near a large feeder stream that tumbled under the ice. The reason for my good luck was obvious; plenty of oxygen-rich water kept the lake recharged at that localized spot.

A great bait for under-ice brookies is a garden worm, or red worm. Anglers who are enterprising can keep worms alive right through the winter season, or they can order them through mail order houses that advertise in magazines. More information on worms is given in another chapter.

Brown Trout

No trout in America possesses the wariness of the brown trout (*Salmo trutta*). This fish is not native, but was introduced to America in 1883 from its European origin. The brown sports black spots over golden-brown flanks, and often has a rich yellow belly. The coloration of a brown, like that of other trout, varies with its environment. Stream and lake fish may look like two different species when compared side-by-side.

Since brown trout are largely nocturnal in their feeding habits, knowledgeable ice anglers pursue them long after the sun disappears over the horizon. This seems strange because one would expect the fish to feed during the day, since water is relatively dark under the ice. To a certain extent this is true, but the bigger fish still prefer to feed during the evening hours.

Few anglers go for browns exclusively because they're so unpredictable. Many are taken by night fishermen who are trying for walleyes, burbot, or smelt. Even under the ice, the brown seems to uphold his reputation of being the smartest trout of all.

Browns feed heavily on small fish, especially in lakes. A minnow-baited rig is often the best offering. I like to use chubs; these fish are durable and stay lively under the ice for long periods of time. I've seen chubs remain fresh and skittery for six to seven hours at a time when hooked lightly behind the dorsal fin. If bait isn't available, my next choice is a big silver jigging spoon. I give it a lot of action because browns seem to prefer it that way.

It's generally agreed that browns are repelled by heavy lines, so I use limber eight-pound test monofilament. By so doing, I can handle nearly anything that comes along if I play it gingerly enough.

Browns prefer to hug the bottom. This is undoubtedly their natural instinct, since they are known to stay close to cover. In lakes with steep sides that slope sharply into the water, browns often cruise along the walls 10 to 20 feet down. In situations like this I've cut holes five feet from shore and fished in water 40 feet deep. Since the browns can be anywhere, I vary the depth of my offering anywhere from 10 feet down to the bottom.

Don't be disappointed if browns ignore your offering. Persistence is the name of the game with these fish wherever they're found.

Lake Trout

The lake trout (*Salvelinus namaycush*) is the granddaddy of our trout. Fish over 100-pounds have been unofficially reported, and 30 to 40 pounders are not uncommon in some of the bigger Canadian lakes.

The laker, which has gray flanks covered with pale spots, is a resident of deep, cold lakes. If you speak of him in New England and eastern Canada, you'd call him a togue. If you're in central Canada, you'll know him as a gray trout. In the west, he's a Mackinaw. Whatever he's called, the lake trout is a highly specialized fish, and he must be pursued in a specialized way. Very few lake trout are taken accidentally. Those who catch him know his habits and habitat.

Lake trout are a good quarry for icefishermen. During the winter, anglers have the advantage of walking over the top of a frozen lake and trying for the big trout from the very roof of his home. As luck would have it, lakers are willing to please in the winter, and provide plenty of sport and action for anglers who go through the trouble of seeking him.

Three important facts should be remembered when fishing for lake trout through the ice. First, the fish are almost always in very deep water. Depending on the lake, proper fishing depths can vary between 30 and 200 feet. The average is somewhere between 50 and 80 feet. Second, lake trout are big. Fifteen-pound fish may be ho-hum in some lakes, and 20-pounders may be more like it. Third, lake trout live in an almost ink-black world. Studies show that in open water, light penetration below 50 feet is extremely low. Ice and snow cover diminish light even further.

This means that an icefisherman must recognize all three facts and apply them to his fishing technique. He must have a high-capacity reel that will hold adequate amounts of line; he must have strong line that will withstand the heavy weight of the quarry; and he should use a flashy lure combined with plenty of action to attract the trout in his twilight world. Only then will an angler have a fighting chance of landing our biggest trout.

It's interesting to note that lake trout prefer specific depths in individual lakes. The act of merely fishing bottom in deep water doesn't always elicit a strike. This behavior may be related to the always-critical oxygen supply, as well as the availability of forage fish. Whatever the case, knowledge of the productive zone in a given lake allows the angler the opportunity of doing some predicting. By obtaining a depth contour chart of the lake, the fisherman can pinpoint specific sites that fall into the prime fishing levels. For example, if lake trout seem to be consistently caught at a depth of 65 feet, all areas in the lake between 60 and 70 feet should be marked on the chart. From that point on, it's a matter of finding the general spots on the lake, then zeroing in with either an electronic depth finder or a weight that's lowered to the bottom. This theory has more going for it than casual observation. Open water trollers know that every lake has certain "runs" that are consistently productive for lake trout. By lining up their boats between two shoreline points, they stay on the "run" and invariably take lakers when they might fail just a few yards off. Close observation of these "runs" reveals that they're virtually the same depth throughout the lake.

Equipment for lake trout varies with the region being fished. Some anglers prefer short, stiff action rods, and others make do with conventional jigging poles. In parts of the Lake States, veteran lake trout fishermen use a "chugging stick." This is a wooden device that is notched at each end. When a fish is hooked, it is retrieved by winding the line inside the notches.

Another variation is the paddleboard, which I've seen used in both the East and West. This wooden device is also hand-held, but the line is recovered by "figure eighting" it from one side of the paddleboard to the other. Copper line is standard equipment on the paddleboard, since it winds well and sinks quickly. The terminal end of this rig includes six feet of 15 or 20-pound test monofilament tied to the copper line. The copper line should never be wound in one piece on the paddleboard, but should be spliced every 50 feet. This is essential to prevent kinking and twisting. At each splice, the line should be secured to a No. 2 swivel.

Terminal rigging for lake trout includes everything from live minnows to assorted lures. If minnows are used, they should be lively and must remain fresh for long periods of time while hooked. Medium to large minnows are the rule, with five-inchers standard fare in many areas. Since these large bait have plenty of pulling power, they must be suspended far enough off the bottom so as not to become tangled in bottom debris. The trick is to keep them swimming free a foot or so off the bottom.

All types of lures are used to fish for lake trout, but most anglers agree that the flashiest, liveliest ones will work best. The Swedish Pimple is an excellent choice, and the balanced minnow-like jigging lures by Rapala are quickly becoming a favorite as well. Mepps spoons, Dardevles, and several others are used with success.

Since lake trout use their olfactory organs to help locate food in the dark environment in which they live, many anglers add a chunk of fish flesh to their lure. In fishermen's lingo, this is referred to as "cut bait" or a "sweetener." Of all the varieties of cut baits, a strip of sucker meat is undoubtedly the most popular across the country. (Chapter 9 on baits gives details on cut bait.) In New England, anglers often fish for lake trout with just cut bait.

A chunk of fish flesh is impaled on a hook and jigged off bottom. An interesting variation is to rig a cut bait on a tip-up and allow it to remain suspended off the bottom or else on the bottom itself. Even though it isn't moving, lakers will readily smell it and strike, regardless of the lack of action.

A 49-day study of icefishermen on two New Hampshire lakes revealed interesting results on the use of baits and lures. On Winnipesaukee Lake, 611 anglers used live bait and caught 148 lake trout; 60 anglers used cut bait and caught 9 lake trout, and 7 fishermen used lures and caught one lake trout. On Newfound Lake, 154 fishermen used cut bait and caught 18 lake trout, 41 anglers used live bait and caught 11 lake trout, and only 1 angler used lures but caught nothing.

The study indicates that most of the Winnipesaukie anglers favored live bait and succeeded in catching the most fish on a percentage basis. On Newfound Lake, fishermen preferred cut baits, but those using live bait were again able to catch more fish, percentagewise.

It should be remembered that this study is applicable only to the lakes in question. As already suggested in chapters 1 and 2, each lake is a separate entity and fish may not react the same way everywhere. The study also didn't involve enough lure fishermen to obtain a valid statistical sample. Perhaps if several hundred anglers used lures, the story would have ended differently. Be that as it may, lake trout can be taken on a variety of offerings. It's up to you to find the best one.

Except in some larger Canadian lakes, lake trout are seldom

known for their ease of catchability. Most anglers who seek them resolve themselves to the fact that they must "put in their time" for a fish, or even a strike. The same New Hampshire study mentioned above showed that the average lake trout angler on Winnipesaukee Lake had to fish 10.38 hours to catch one lake trout. Newfound Lake fishermen fished an average of 16 hours to catch one lake trout.

Although this data suggests that lake trout fishermen who wish to be successful must also be persistent, it points out that fishing for these big trout can be mighty slow with long waits between bites. Yet, in every study made that breaks down fishing success by hours spent fishing, it isn't mentioned that most of these fish are taken by a relatively small percentage of the total angler population. In other words, a few veterans take most of the fish. That's why it's important to pay attention to details in every aspect of icefishing. Whether you're after lake trout in Jackson Lake, Wyoming; Green Lake, Wisconsin; or Lake Winnipesaukee, prepare yourself fully for our biggest trout. You'll be rewarded many times over if you do.

When the "reward" is about to become a reality, inexperienced anglers botch up the situation by letting excitement get the best of themselves. Keep your cool when you find a lake trout on the end of the line. After setting the hook hard, let the fish take all the line he wants, but keep a good steady tension on it by allowing it to slide through your fingers if you're using a tip-up. If you're using a reel, let him fight the drag as you would in open water. When he's played out a good share of line and reduced his pulling antics, retrieve the line slowly and coax him toward the hole. After a few initial bursts of action, he'll tire and yield to your demands quickly. But don't be disillusioned. When he sees the hole and where he's headed, he'll go through another series of evasive maneuvers. Now comes the moment of truth, the time when it becomes necessary to remove the fish from the water and onto the ice. The amateur will typically look down, spot the big thrashing fish, say "wow, look what I've got," and impulsively try to yank the reluctant quarry through the hole. This seldom works. The tried and true method is to get down on your knees (You might pray a little while you're there.), watch the head of the fish, and carefully coax it toward the hole. This must be done without pause while the fish is still on the way up. When his head is aimed toward the hole, apply all the pressure you dare. With his snout pointed in the direction of the hole, his body thrusts will propel him where you want him—up and out. As he's coming strong, maintain the pressure and lead him bravely through the hole. When he hits the ice, sweep him away from the hole so he can't flop back in.

There is one important rule to remember. Always be sure the hole is big enough to comfortably maneuver a fish through it. This doesn't mean you need an opening big enough to fit a 55-gallon drum through—just big enough for a healthy fish. A 6-inch hole for yellow perch and panfish won't handle many lakers. Go to an 8-inch bore or bigger—and be sure to comply with your state's regulations since many have restrictions on maximum hole size.

How To Catch Panfish

Fishing Fun For Everyone

The term panfish is generally considered to include several species of freshwater fish that are too small to be regarded as gamefish. For the purposes of this book, we'll discuss in detail the Big Three of the panfish family—the bluegill, yellow perch, and crappie. Each of these species is responsible for millions of angler days every icefishing season. Other panfish that are taken regularly through the ice, will be covered, too. They include the pumpkinseed sunfish, white bass, white perch, rock bass, smelt, and bullhead.

This angler has made tracks to a favorite winter sport. He's trying for panfish in a Michigan lake. *Photo courtesy of Michigan Travel Commission.*

Although panfish can hardly be classed as glamour species, they nonetheless are the drawing cards that attract countless anglers from their warm homes onto frozen lakes. The only thing fishermen ask in return is a bit of action and perhaps a quarter-bucket of fish that they can take home to convert into a tasty treat. And treat they are! No fish are more succulent than panfish, especially in the winter, when their flesh is firm and nutty. It's no wonder that more people are trying icefishing each year. With millions of panfish lurking under the ice of practically every lake, who can ignore the sport or the fish?

Bluegills

The bluegill (*Lepomis macrochirus*) is the undisputed champion of the American fisherman. It's been said that more anglers fish for bluegills than any other species. This beautiful fish is dark olive green on the back, has a blue iridescent sheen on the sides, and is marked with several dark bands that run vertically down each side. A black ear flap located on the tip of each gill plate is characteristic of the species.

Although its original range included much of central and eastern America, the bluegill has been introduced into all of the lower 48 states. The reasons for its popularity are obvious. The little fish is an angler's delight because it hits practically everything offered—with gusto. Flies, poppers, small spoons, spinners, and baits,—are all enthusiastically accepted by bluegills. Its sporty fight makes it a top quarry for the light-tackle enthusiast. Finally, there's no better gastronomical delight when bluegill fillets are sautéed golden brown in a light butter sauce.

Bluegills were not a part of the icefishing scene a few decades ago. There were plenty of fish around, but few anglers knew how to catch them. The story goes that a handful of Old World immigrants in the Lake States used mysterious little jigs and caught bushels of bluegills on them. Word spread quickly, and the funny lures were suddenly in great demand. Eventually the lures were manufactured for a mass market, and now a number of companies make several varieties. All sizes, shapes, and colors are now available in sporting goods stores where icefishing is popular.

The lures, which are generally between one and two inches long, are just the ticket for little bluegill mouths and appetites. They're

Bluegills are a favorite quarry among icefishermen everywhere. This angler took his fish on an ice fly. *Photo courtesy of Merritt Benson.*

small and flashy, and several have little plastic appendages that flip around as the lure is jigged. The bluegills love 'em! Some of the more popular models are the Russian Hook, Swedish Pimple, and teardrop. All are proven bluegill killers and have undoubtedly accounted for more than a few bluegill dinners.

I was introduced to bluegills through the ice by the late Charlie Booth, a wonderful gentleman from Highland Falls, New York. During his retirement, Charlie spent every possible day fishing, and icefishing was his favorite of all.

Until I met Charlie, my total icefishing experiences involved tip-up fishing for pickerel, northern pike, crappies, and yellow perch. I had yet to graduate to the little jigging rods that were beginning to show up on the ice.

It didn't take long for Charlie to win me over as a convert. Every time I spotted him on the ice he had big messes of bluegills lying around him, as well as perch and crappies. But bluegills were his chief quarry.

Left: A bluegill is coaxed through an ice hole after hitting an ice fly. Bluegills are highly selective in the winter and are attracted to small lures and flies sweetened with a larva. *Photo courtesy of Merritt Benson.*

Right: A jigging rod, an ice fly, and an auger are all that you need in order to catch a nice mess of winter bluegills. Most anglers who fish for bluegills agree that many holes may need to be cut to find the fish.

Somehow, Charlie had obtained a few of the Russian Hooks that were just beginning to appear in the Midwest. Being the innovative person he was, he went to work in his basement and hammered out several handmade replicas. They worked just as well as the originals, and we continued to take as many bluegills as we wanted.

As the years passed, I gained more and more knowledge observing and listening to Charlie and his fishing buddies. I put their advice into practice wherever I went, and added a few new tricks that came with experience.

The bluegill isn't difficult to catch under the ice, but there are some important do's and dont's to follow when pursuing these gamey little fish. This fish is a very delicate biter in the winter. Light lines, tiny lures, and small bobbers are the rule if one wants to collect as many fish as he can.

On some days, the typical bluegill bite may be a mere nudge that can scarcely be seen. Only the most attentive angler can recognize the strike. Once, while I was fishing for bluegills in New York, the fish bit so lightly that the only way I could see the strike was to get down on my hands and knees and watch my line. I didn't use a bobber, and the only way I could get the fish to hit was to allow the baited jig to rest quietly on the bottom. By positioning my head a foot or so from the hole, I watched the line that floated on its surface. When the line dipped or twitched just a fraction, I grabbed the entire coil and jerked the bait with a sharp snap. Invariably I'd hook a bluegill, and when I went home I had a mess of fish that was as impressive as any I'd ever seen. Some were better than nine inches long—a big bluegill anywhere! The offering I used that day is the same I use everywhere for winter bluegills. It's a yellow, tear-drop jig baited with a mousee grub. If that combination doesn't take bluegills, then I switch to a different colored tear-drop, usually green, then to the fluorescent colors if green doesn't work.

I'm not a "purist" icefisherman. I use some kind of bait on my lures in almost every instance. There are some folks who take pride in catching fish through the ice without the aid of baits, and I admire their good sporting values and skills. But I'm not one of them. I'm an opportunist, and I'll slap anything that's legal on my lure to put more fish on the ice. When it comes to bluegills, I honestly believe that the addition of a grub or larvae is the key to success. (The chapter on baits will discuss the baits that are available to icefishermen.)

Bluegills are most commonly found in water 15 to 25 feet deep. I begin looking for fish by cutting holes near the points of peninsulas or islands. These areas usually indicate a drop-off zone where bluegills tend to congregate. A good rule of thumb is to seek under-ice bluegills in the same areas where they were found during the dog days of summer. Generally speaking, that area will be in excess of 15 feet in depth.

If bluegills don't bite as soon as I start fishing, I never leave the ice during the winter. They tend to stay put for long periods of time. caught fish through that particular hole a day or two before. Chances are good that the fish are down there but might not be interested in the bait I'm using. Bluegills aren't known to move much under the ice during the winter, but tend to stay put for long periods of time. If I've fished the hole for 10 minutes with 3 different lures and there is still no action, I'll pick up and move off to another spot. But I won't move far. Thirty to 50 feet is about maximum, since the fish are likely to be somewhere in the general vicinity.

Bluegills may not always be just off the bottom, although that's generally where they're found. Occasionally the fish are suspended somewhere between the floor of the lake and the ice layer. This is especially noticeable in shallow depths, although it sometimes occurs in deeper waters, too. Since bluegills school in bunches, it goes without saying that a fish caught at a certain level is an indicator that the rest of the school is there, too. Adjust your techniques to the level that produced fish, even though it's "correct" to fish off bottom. Remember, the best depth to fish is the one where the fish are living at that particular time.

Bluegills tend to school according to uniform sizes. I've found that most of the fish that come out of a hole are about the same size, and only if I move to another hole will I catch bigger or smaller fish. This isn't always the case, but it's happened enough that I believe it.

When I find productive holes, I mark them before I leave so I can find them the next time I fish. A snowstorm between visits can easily blot out a favorite hole that was consistently good to me. I found that the best way to mark a hole is to stick a branch into the snow or slush adjacent to it. That way I can find the hole regardless of the snow cover later on.

It's often productive to return to the precise spot that produced before. Here's why. Take a good close look across a frozen lake and interpret what you can see. To put it simply—nothing, except ice and snow, and a very barren landscape at that. Now look at the holes drilled and chopped by anglers—do you see anything else? Again, nothing else is evident except a frozen, sterile, lifeless scene. But now use your imagination and look *under* those holes. Picture the lake bottom and everything that might be going on down there. Just because the holes look alike from the top doesn't mean they have the same structure and environment under them. Certainly not! The lake floor is covered with trees, stumps, reefs, drop-offs, sandy bars, weed patches, perhaps even road beds, root cellars, and fence posts. Every hole has its own little world under it, and that might be just the spot where the bluegills are living. For that reason, a "hot" hole might be just that—if you've drilled it in just the right place. If that's the case, it would be foolish to lose it if you don't have to.

Bluegills are known to stunt badly in overpopulated lakes. Since they're so prolific, they reproduce rapidly and soon exceed the ability of the lake to adequately support them. Predation by larger fish doesn't always help to thin the populations, because bluegills are surprisingly furtive and not easy to catch. This being the case, anglers are doing the lake and the fish a favor by keeping every bluegill they catch. Biologists admit that few, if any, bluegill lakes have ever been overfished to the point where the harvest was detrimental to the overall bluegill population.

Bag limits are often imposed on bluegills to distribute the catch over a greater number of anglers rather than to protect the species. Even so, most limits are extremely liberal, and a knowledgeable fisherman seldom has trouble taking what he needs.

Thanks to the cooperative nature of the bluegill, he reigns supreme in most of the lakes across America.

Yellow Perch

The yellow perch (*Perca flavescens*), is one of the main reasons why millions of people flock to frozen lakes each winter. During a winter study on the Canadian portion of Lake Erie, some 56,000 ice anglers harvested over 1.8 million yellow perch. This averaged out to almost 40 fish per angler, which isn't a bad haul for a day on the ice.

The yellow perch, which has a striking yellow body with dark vertical bars, is built to tolerate this kind of pressure. Females are extremely prolific and can lay up to 75,000 eggs each spring. Although predation on young perch is substantial, enough survive to maintain high numbers. Overpopulation is a common problem, and fishing is often inadequate to keep the populations thinned to healthy levels. But sometimes it is. For example, it's been estimated that each acre of 10,000-acre Lake Mendota, Wisconsin, produces 40 pounds of chunky perch. Some biologists theorize that this exceptional harvest helps the overall fish population by keeping them thinned to adequate levels where the lake can support them.

Each perch lake has its own unique fish population with individual pecularities and characteristics. In some lakes, perch are jumbos and seem to remain that way with amazing consistency. In other lakes, a 12-inch fish is a trophy. The health and welfare of a fish population depends on many factors. With perch as well as most others, lake fertility and predation is a key factor. Fertile lakes with good walleye populations, for example, might support big perch since walleyes prey almost exclusively on perch whenever they're available. Young perch are excellent prey species, because they aren't protected by their parents after hatching but swim about in large schools. If enough predators are present in the lake community, they'll make quick inroads into the schools of slow-swimming perch. Surviving

Jeff Pavia hoists a good yellow perch from a lake in New York State. Jeff favors meal worms for perch, and he likes to attach one to a Swedish Pimple. Note the packbasket for carrying gear.

perch will therefore have less competition and grow more rapidly. If predators are lacking, however, the perch quickly take over the lake and make heavy demands on the food supply. When this supply can no longer keep the perch nourished adequately, the fish grow slowly and become stunted.

As it is, perch grow slowly in northern latitudes, even when the food supply is adequate. Under normal conditions, a yellow perch will grow three inches in its first year. By the second year it will be 6 inches long, and 8 inches the third year. Thus, a 10-inch perch that wiggles up through a hole in the ice will be four or five years old. Of course, the rate of growth in any given lake depends on a number of environmental factors.

There are a few scattered lakes that support very few perch, but the ones that are in them are granddaddies. I know a small lake in New York which gives up only 6 to 10 perch each winter, but none of them are under 2 pounds. The lake, which is only about 15 acres, is fished mostly by youngsters who board at a nearby youth camp in the summer. Each winter, 3 or 4 of us would walk in to the lake and try for a big perch exclusively. We used tip-ups and big minnows, since live baits under 3 inches didn't seem to arouse the interest of the lunker perch. If we caught only one fish a day, the outing was a success. The huge perch were often in excess of 16 inches.

But for every lake with giant perch, there are dozens with small to medium fish. This doesn't deter most anglers, though, because 8

Left: Jerry Horgesheimer, a resident of Ogden, Utah, tussles with a perch in Utah's Yuba Lake. The fish were taken at the bottom of the lake in 60 feet of water. Perch eyes were the best bait.

Right: A native Midwesterner now living in the West, Horgesheimer was delighted to find that he could catch chunky perch like these in Western waters.

to 12-inch fish are just as tasty as the bigger ones. They're easier to catch, too.

If there's a single rule for winter perch fishing, it has to be this: To find the fish, locate the deepest water in the lake and cut your hole right over it. If oxygen is sufficient, yellow perch will be down as far as they can get, even as far as 60 feet. I fish a Western lake for perch where the deepest depth is about 65 feet. That's the spot where all the perch are caught. It's interesting to note that fish taken at this depth undergo a rapid rate of pressure change on the way up. So much so, in fact, that their stomachs actually protrude from their mouths when they appear at the hole. As a humane gesture, I rap each fish smartly over the head with the handle of my ice skimmer, even though they appear to be practically dead when they're lifted onto the ice.

There are exceptions to the rule about perch being in the deepest part of the lake. These fish are on the move frequently under the ice, and travel in large schools. It's no surprise when they move from a depth of 50 feet to 35 feet. A wise angler will try other areas when no bites are forthcoming in spots that normally produce. As a matter of fact, it's been reported that yellow perch make daily migrations under the ice. Schools of fish allegedly move toward the shallows during the dark hours, and then back out to the deep water during the daytime. I've seen instances where this appeared to be true. Early-morning anglers who fished near shore in about 20 feet of water had good perch action from daylight until about 8 o'clock in the morning. After 8 the fishing all but stopped while anglers over deep water (40 feet) began catching fish.

In lakes that are of a fairly uniform depth, perch may mix with bluegills. This is especially true in lakes that are fairly shallow—8 to 20 feet deep.

No ice angler cuts more holes than the perch fisherman. As soon as the veteran angler hits the ice, he begins cutting as many holes as he can. This might amount to as many as 20 to 30 if he has a power auger and/or a strong back.

Here's how an experienced perch fisherman spends a day on the lake. After cutting several holes, he unlimbers his favorite jigging rod and ties on a small spoon or jig. If he's a purist he'll use a lure with no bait attached. If he doesn't care about such things, he'll impale a mealworm, waxworm, mousee, or other larvae on his lure. With the lure tied on firmly, he plops it into the hole, allowing it to sink to the bottom. When the line stops feeding into the hole, he reels in slowly until the line straightens, indicating that he's taken in all the slack between the rod and lure. With the lure barely resting on bottom, he jigs the rod according to the technique he likes best. Some fishermen use a long, upward sweep, others jiggle the lure rapidly, and still others twitch it every few seconds. Indeed, every angler has his own style, and many change their jigging tempo or rhythm if the bites are slow in coming. Most perch bites come when the lure is falling, so the fisherman must pay attention to his jigging efforts.

Yellow perch have a varied diet, and are highly predatory. Small minnows are ideal baits, and are commonly used with tip-ups, especially in the northeast.

Yellow perch are school fish, and I set the devices over a wide area, rather than a localized spot. That way I'll have a better chance of finding a school. When one of my flags wave and show me where the fish are, I'll move other tip-ups closer to the action. I prefer to circle the hot hole with the other tip-ups. In this manner I can cover much of the school. As a rule, I don't cut a new hole any closer than 20 feet from the active hole. Perch schools often extend a long way under the ice.

Since I like to use a jigging rod as well as tip-ups, I normally set all my devices and then jig while waiting for a flag to fly. Of course, the jigging rod takes the place of a tip-up, so in states that allow five lines per angler, only four tip-ups can be used if the angler wants to jig.

One advantage of jigging while using tip-ups is that the lure on the jig pole might find fish faster than minnows, especially if the angler is fishing several holes. When that happens, the tip-ups can be moved to the area where the perch have been located.

While some believe that unbaited lures are as effective for perch as baited lures, I'll stand by the Missouri attitude—"show-me." One day I had a contest with a companion to see who could catch the most yellow perch. We stood side-by-side and fished holes that were just two feet apart. Our lines and lures were exactly the same, and we jigged alike. However, he was using a mealworm impaled on his lure while I left mine unbaited. There was no contest. He outfished me completely, even though we switched holes constantly. Then, to prove the point, I hooked a mealworm on my line and he fished his without. The tables turned immediately! In no time I had the great bulk of fish flopping on the ice. Though a sweetener might not *always* succeed, the odds are always better when a bit of meat is added to the lure.

This section on yellow perch fishing wouldn't be complete if I didn't mention the use of perch eyes for bait. As long as there are perch fishermen, there will be people using perch eyes. They work so well that many anglers use them on a plain hook fished just off the bottom.

The technique in obtaining and using eyes is simple. Of course, one must first have a perch before obtaining a perch eye. Once a fish is caught, kill it and slide a thumbnail into the socket and under the entire eyeball. Apply gentle pressure until the eye pops away from the head completely. The idea is to remove the entire eye so it is intact and not squeezed of its fluids. Applying the eye to the hook is easy. Merely impale the hook through it, again taking care not to squeeze too hard. The hooks's point should be pushed far enough through the eye so that it barely emerges from the other side. Once

Author shows a dandy pair of yellow perch that were taken on a Swedish Pimple in 50 feet of water. The perch are females and contain delicious roe.

the eye is on the hook, the rest is up to the perch below the ice. If they're typical, they'll keep you supplied with all the fresh eyes you need, since one eye on a hook begets two more each time a fish hits the ice!

Yellow perch often travel in schools of the same sex, especially in winter. On more than one ocassion I've taken nothing but female fish. In fact, I've caught mostly females through the ice, and very few males. Females will invariably have distended bellies full of roe during the winter fishing season. When I was a youngster I was disturbed at killing fish laden with eggs. Now I can appreciate the fact that I'm actually doing the population a favor by removing a potential breeder.

Perch roe is a delicacy, and in my family it's as desirable as perch flesh. I like to make "roecakes," and then fry them. To do this, I remove the membrane that holds the roe in a sac, and mix the loose roe with a beaten egg and a bit of milk. Then I simply fry the batter as I would flapjacks. A better repast is hard to find, but this is just one of the many delights of yellow-perch icefishing.

Crappies

There are two species of crappies in the United States: the black crappie (*Pomoxis nigromaculatus*), and the white crappie (*Pomoxis annularis*). The black crappie is basically a fish of the North, where it prefers clear, cool lakes and rivers. The white crappie can tolerate more turbid waters and is generally a Southern fish, although it has been introduced to waters throughout the north. Ice fishermen lump the two together and make no distinction as to species. All are known simply as crappies (or "croppies", a popular pronunciation in many areas).

These Utah anglers are fishing for crappies under the towering Wasatch Mountain Range. Westerners are as enthusiastic about the sport as are their Eastern brethren.

A Minnesota angler unhooks a nice crappie that took his minnow. For best results on crappies, minnows should be small—about two to three inches long. *Photo courtesy of Bob Gilsvik.*

Crappies are striking fish, especially in the breeding season when their colors are most pronounced. They have a mottled appearance with black-green specks and bands over silver flanks. Large dorsal and anal fins give them a flowing appearance, and their small head makes the rest of the body appear larger than it is.

They eat nearly any live food, including crustaceans, all forms of insects, and fish. Icefishermen take them on an assortment of hardware, but minnows seem to be the top crappie bait.

The angling fraternity generally views the crappie as a springtime fish that is exclusively pursued adjacent to downed trees, waterlogged brush, and flooded forests.

The winter fisherman knows better. Crappies cooperate beautifully under the ice, and knowledgeable anglers take home dandy messes of these tasty fish. There are some differences in crappie fishing, compared to other panfish fishing, however.

A primary difference is the feeding time of the crappie. Whereas bluegills and yellow perch bite all day, crappies might not begin until dusk. This is especially true in late winter.

I learned about evening fishing for crappies on an Eastern lake. Light was fading fast as I walked off the lake. Since I was too young to drive, I left the ice early because I had a long walk home. I reached the shore and met three men who were just heading onto the ice. They carried lanterns, and I couldnt imagine what they were going to do. I recognized one as a local bait dealer and asked what he was going to fish for. When he said crappies I thought he was joking, but he told me to check at the gas station where he worked when I walked home from school the next day. I did, and he showed me the heads of 18 huge crappies. I restructured my fishing schedule at that point and stayed on the ice as long as I could every day I fished. My luck changed and I began to take home bragging-size crappies.

I witnessed a similar experience on Willard Bay, a Utah impoundment that suddenly became a popular crappie spot during winter, 1977. Although crappies had been taken by open-water anglers prior to then, it wasn't a winter fishery until a few diehard anglers successfully tried icefishing and caught all the fish they wanted. Word spread quickly, and in just one month 25,000 anglers converged on the lake. Most of them knew nothing about icefishing for crappies. During the first week of fishing, only a handful of people stayed out on the ice after the sun went down. Most of them were Midwesterners who were stationed at a nearby air force base. Slowly, word got around and local residents were beginning to stick it out a little longer on the ice. Before the month was over, several hundred people fished Willard Bay every evening long after the sun went down.

One of the Midwesterners who fished Willard Bay was Wayne Nicolls, a native of Chippewa Falls, Wisconsin. Wayne worked as a public information officer for the U.S. Forest Service in Ogden, and was absolutely delighted to live close to a crappie lake. When he transferred to Utah from the Lake States he almost left his icefishing gear back home, but he brought it along.

I fished with Wayne on Willard Bay, and quickly learned that he was a pro at catching crappies. Wherever he fished, he easily caught three crappies to one of any angler standing anywhere around him. Wayne showed me how he did it. Whenever his bobber moved even a tiny bit, he snapped his jigging rod up to set the hook. In most cases, the sensitive rod bent sharply because he had hooked a feisty crappie. Sometimes the bobber appeared to just slowly drift across the hole as if the breeze were blowing it, but he'd set the hook quickly, and would often get a fish. Wayne told me that crappies often bite delicately, especially when a baited jig is being used. Since Utah law prohibits the use of live minnows for bait, he was using tear-drop jigs, sweetened with a meal worm.

Like yellow perch, crappies can be taken on tip-ups as well as

A mixed bag of panfish. These crappies and bluegills fell for a teardrop lure baited with a mousee larva. *Photo courtesy of Robert Demetry.*

jigging rods. When minnows are used, two to three-inch fish are about the right size.

Crappies aren't wanderers like perch. They generally stay in an area that has preferred habitat. To a crappie, this means underwater debris, vegetation, a sunken tree, or other shelter. Even in winter crappies like to be near broken habitat that offers cover. Therefore, an angler who is knowledgeable of a lake should direct his efforts over areas that produce in the spring, provided they're deep enough.

Don't count on crappies lying on bottom like other fish. In winter, crappies will suspend at any level, and I've seen them consistently attack lures right under the ice just barely down from the hole. I know one angler who swears that a crappie chased his jig right through the hole and iced itself without ever touching the lure.

Crappies also school in the winter. When one fish is caught, unhook it quickly, and get the lure or minnow back down the hole as soon as possible. Stay with the depth that's productive, and check the minnow or bait frequently to be sure they're fresh.

These Eastern anglers fish for panfish during a snowstorm. Note how close they are to shore. Often the shallow shoreline areas are the most productive. *Photo courtesy of Pennsylvania Fish Commission.*

Other Panfish

The white bass (*Roccus chrysops*) is a true bass, and is related to the striped bass, yellow bass, and white perch. This fish has a silvery body with about 10 thin, dark lines that run from gills to tail. The original range of the white bass was from the Great Lakes to Kansas and Missouri, and from the Mississippi to the west slope of the Alleghenies. Today, the species has been stocked extensively throughout America. It is a roaring success in big impoundments. The fish are extremely prolific, with some of the larger females carrying 1 million eggs.

White bass are constant wanderers, and are often a "feast or famine" proposition. They bite well under the ice, and will attack most offerings. Small minnows are always a good bait, with 2-inch shiners being top fare. Jigs are effective for white bass and any kind of added grub or bait keeps action going on a slow day. These fish aren't large, but will usually run an average of 10 to 13 inches in northern waters. They grow fast and are fairly short-lived. They seldom live longer than 5 years.

White perch (*Roccus americanus*) live along the Atlantic seaboard, although there are spotty populations as far inland as the Great Lakes. These fish have silvery green sides, blending into a rich olive or black-green back.

The species lives in salt water as well as brackish and fresh water. White perch reproduce rapidly, and are numerous wherever they're found. Ice anglers take heavy messes of white perch by using small minnows or baits. Any type of larvae on a plain hook is effective under the ice. Since white perch are fond of grubbing larvae out of muddy pond bottoms, fishermen often look for perch over areas of the lake that have a muddy bed. Perch may be at any depth, so wise anglers start at the bottom and work the bait up until fish are located. If action is slow, a move well away from the area is best. One of the best ways to locate a white perch hotspot is to ask a local resident, or watch the concentrations of anglers. The latter technique works well anywhere icefishing is popular. Fishermen will be located where the fish are.

The Rock Bass (*Ambloplites rupestris*) enjoys a fairly large range in the United States. It's found from New England to the Gulf States. It's also called goggle-eye because of its large red eyes. This species has a brassy, olive green color and is shaped like a sunfish. A fairly large mouth allows it to prey on an assortment of creatures.

As its name suggests, the rock bass is fond of rocky, gravely areas. In the winter, they're found over shoals that slope away from peninsulas and irregular shorelines. Many ice fishermen take rock bass incidental to other panfish. Very few anglers pursue them exclusively through the ice.

Bullheads (*Ictalurus*) come in three species; brown, black, and yellow. Each has a slightly different habitat preference, but they're all pretty well mixed around the country. Few people need an introduction to the bullhead since its whiskered face and scaleless body is common in all of the lower 48 states.

The inclusion of these fish in an icefishing book might come as a surprise to some anglers. It's commonly believed that bullheads burrow in the mud during the winter months and lie dormant until spring. This is an old wives' tale. Bullheads are indeed active under the ice, though not to the extent they are in the spring and summer.

I discovered under-ice bullheads while night fishing for walleyes. It was my debut trip for winter walleyes while using specially

Many folks refuse to believe that bullhead catfish bite under the ice. This catfish was taken after dark on a tip-up baited with a minnow. The fisherman was aiming for walleyes.

equipped tip-ups. The devices were fitted with lights that blinked on when a fish took the minnow bait.

My companions and I huddled around a bonfire on shore when the first light winked on far across the lake. It was about 10 P.M., and the temperature was –10° F. We ran across the ice to the tip-up, positive that a walleye had taken the four-inch golden shiner. When my buddy set the hook and hauled in the fish, I was amazed to see a two-pound bullhead on the end of the line. My pals weren't surprised, though. They had commonly caught bullheads before while night icefishing. Before that evening was over, we had taken six more bullheads and four walleyes. Yes, bullheads are indeed alive and well under the ice. It just takes a hardy soul to prove it!

For being such small fish, smelt (*Osmerus mordax*) have a big following. The little fish, which are technically known as rainbow smelt, never fail to attract big crowds when they make themselves available to icefishermen. Interest in them doesn't stop when the ice goes out, either. Millions of fish make spawning runs up little creeks and streams in the spring, and crowds of anglers try for them with dipnets until the last smelt makes its way back down.

When I was living in the Northeast, the high point of every February was to make a smelt trip to Lake Champlain. We planned the event well in advance and reserved a shanty from a local resident who rented a few shanties to out-of-town fishermen. We seldom failed to bring home a good mess of fish on those outings. In productive lakes such as Champlain, all that's required to catch smelt is patience and a soft cushion to sit on. The smelt's small size requires overtime to accumulate enough fish to take home.

Smelt bite at all times, depending on the whim of the fisherman. Since northern nights are cold, a shanty is almost a requirement to stay warm if one elects to fish then. This is especially true because it's necessary to sit in one spot for a long time.

The small size of the fish requires small bait. Smelt are vicious little things, and attack anything they can get into their mouth. Very small minnows are highly effective but it takes a lot of time (and minnows) to keep hooks baited. Most anglers prefer to use a small jig baited with a sliver of smelt skin, or a larvae. To use a piece of smelt for bait, fillet a layer of skin off the side of a smelt with a very sharp knife. With a bit of care, none of the edible flesh need be cut into. I like to use a strip of skin about two inches long, and 1/2-inch wide. I hook it near one of the ends much like a pork rind. It doesn't take long for smelt to chew the skin into tatters, so it'll probably be necessary to use a fresh piece after every two or three fish.

Smelt usually live in the same area of a lake each year, and are nearly always in deep water. However, I've caught them at every depth in a 75-foot lake, even directly under the ice. They'll usually be in the lower half of a lake.

Smelt can be pickled, kippered, smoked, fried—anything goes. They easily make up for their small size when they're heaped in a steaming platter awaiting attention at the dinner table.

How To Catch The Big and Unusual Fish

Walleye

The walleye (*Stizostedion vitreum*) suffers from many untruths. Though widely known as the "walleyed pike," it really isn't a pike. The walleye is actually first cousin to the yellow perch, and is a true member of the perch family. Its common classification as a cold-water fish is another fallacy. Although it prefers cool water, it's really a warm-water species.

Now let's look at some truths about the walleye. It's considered to provide *the* very best eating of all the freshwater fish in North America. I've never met a person who has eaten walleye that ranks it second, or even comparable, to another fish. Another plus is the walleye's pleasing disposition toward icefishermen. The fish is quite at home under the ice and is active enough to tighten lines across the northern tier of the country. Thus, there's no question that this fish has a widespread fan club in the winter time.

The walleye is a longish, gray-green fish with huge eyes and a toothy mouth. Its physical makeup immediately indicates two characteristics of the species: it is largely nocturnal, (thus the big eyes); and it eats lots of little fish (thus the big teeth). Those two clues tell the basic story on how to catch it.

A big, lively minnow is one of the best baits for winter walleyes. Three to five-inch shiners or chubs are preferred baits, especially where walleye run to good sizes. Five-pound walleyes are nice fish around anybody's ice holes, and the norm is more like two to three-pounders. Fish in the seven and eight-pound class are trophies and should be photographed for the family scrapbook.

Walleyes are naturals for tip-up fishermen. They inhale minnows and usually make a long, smooth run after the flag is tripped. Walleyes are sometimes hard to find under the ice because they're school fish; they travel often from one part of the lake to another. Tip-ups are silent fishermen that patiently wait until the walleyes decide to swim near enough to see the minnow offering.

I've been told by fisheries biologists that walleyes normally swim around a lake roughly parallel to the shoreline. With that bit of knowledge, I pattern my tip-ups in a straight line perpendicular to the shoreline. That way a school of walleyes coming around will be sure to bump into one of my baits somewhere along the route. I space the tip-ups about 25 feet apart. This makes it difficult for fish to pass between two baits without noticing them.

Walleyes are usually bottom fish. The only time I've ever seen them behave differently is during warm summer evenings when they occasionally smack surface plugs being fished for bass. For best results in the winter, the minnow should be fished just barely off the bottom where the walleyes travel.

There's a trick to finding the right depth every time a minnow is dunked into an ice hole. Use a small clamp-on depth finder to determine the water depth. The procedure goes like this: The depth finder, which is merely a weight with an alligator-like clamp attached to it, is pinched to the bare hook. The terminal rig is tossed into the hole. The weight quickly sinks to the bottom and stops abruptly when it hits. At this point, the line is slowly raised until the bottom is precisely located. With this done, the angler marks the line so the bait will rest about 8 to 12 inches off the bottom. The best way to mark the line is to slide a button along the line and stop it at the correct area. Of course, the button must be placed on the line before the hook and shot is attached. With the button or other mark in the proper area, the tip-up can be set correctly every time without requiring the angler to determine the right depth each time the minnow is lowered.

Walleyes are nocturnal; the best icefishing for them is during the evening hours. Enough fish are still taken during daytime by winter anglers to make it worthwhile. In lakes where it's legal to leave tip-ups unattended, some anglers make good walleye catches by baiting their tip-ups with fresh minnows just before dark, leaving them overnight, and checking them the next morning. A good share of their lines hold walleyes when they chop out the frozen tip-ups. There's some question as to the sporting etiquette of this technique, but it puts fillets in the freezer. A better way is to use specialized tip-ups outfitted with lights that blink on when a fish trips the trigger. These devices can be purchased from several mail-order houses and

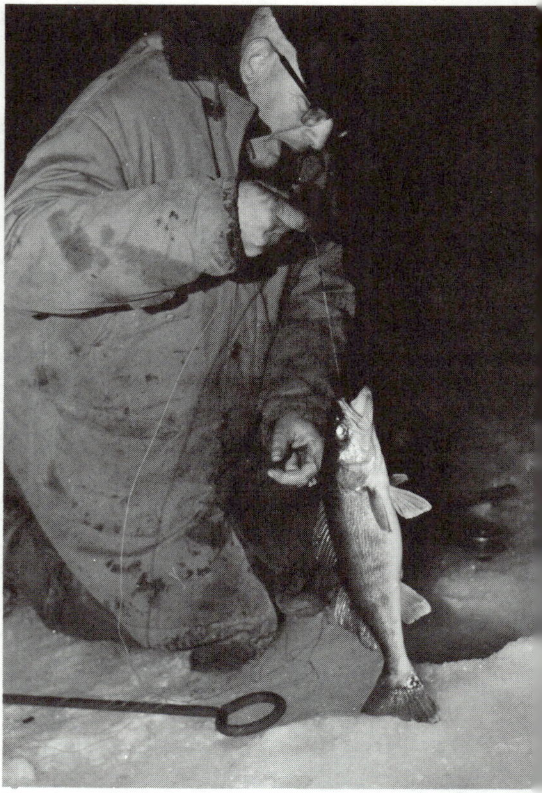

Left: This night fisherman waits for a walleye to run with the bait before setting the hook. Walleyes occasionally will mouth a bait before moving off with it.

Right: Walleyes readily bite at night and are taken by tip-up fishermen who are willing to brave the cold. This walleye was taken shortly after midnight on a New York State lake.

sporting goods stores. There's plenty of camaraderie and yarn-spinning when a bunch of people huddle around a hot fire waiting for lights to flick on in the inky blackness.

Walleyes hit lures well, and are a popular quarry for anglers who like to use jigging rods. Silver spoons are standard fare, although the horizontal minnow plugs that appear on the ice more frequently these days are highly effective, too. Bucktail and marabou jigs are good, and are usually bounced on the bottom so they make little puffs of muddy water when they hit. Although walleyes aren't known for their fighting ability, they're known to really wallop lures when they hit.

Walleyes like rocky areas, and are usually found over shoals in moderately deep water. Most of them are taken in water 15 to 30 feet deep. Many lakes have favored "walleye grounds" where the fish are prevalent.

Few knowledgeable walleye fishermen expect to catch a lot of fish when the sun shines brightly. When that happens, they move to deeper water and rig up for yellow perch since the two species are usually found together in the same lakes. At dusk, the fishermen move toward the shoals and try for walleyes.

Although walleyes are best-known in the Lake States and Canada, extensive plantings in the West have resulted in excellent populations in many places. Anglers in Wyoming, Colorado, Montana, and other Western states enjoy this delectable fish as much as other warm-water species. At one time, trout were the only species a Westerner could pursue, but that's all changed. Varied fish species are now available to anglers no matter where they live.

Saugers are close relatives to walleyes. They live in huge impoundments and natural lakes. The two fish look so much alike that it's often difficult to tell them apart. Walleyes, however, carry a telltale white mark at the base of their tail fin. Saugers have no such mark. Another way is by checking the spiny dorsal fin on the back of the fish. If it's a sauger, it'll have two or three rows of black dots on it.

Saugers aren't nearly as big as walleyes, but their flesh is comparable. A big sauger will be three or four pounds, with most running one to two pounds.

Saugers behave pretty much like walleyes, so the same techniques prevail. The only difference might be to use slightly smaller minnows and lures.

Eastern Chain Pickerel

The chain pickerel (*Esox niger*) is the fish I grew up with in the Northeast. I have always respected it, especially in my boyhood when the long green fish seemed so vicious and malevolent.

Three species of pickerel are found in the United States: the chain, the grass and redfin species. The two latter fish are relatively unimportant to icefishermen since they hardly grow to eating size. They deserve mention, however, because there are a few localized areas where these fish are taken by winter anglers.

Chain pickerel reside along the Atlantic seaboard. They range

Steve Macica rushes to a tip-up that waves its flag, signaling that a fish has taken the bait. With a little luck, Steve will haul a pickerel out of this New York lake.

from Canada down through Florida, and extend inland to the Allegheny Mountains. Pickerel are abundant in southern Maine, Massachusetts, Connecticut, southern New York, and New Jersey. They're found near high-population areas, so many anglers seek them.

The pickerel is an ominous-looking fish, resembling his close cousins—the northern pike and muskellunge. The body is long and streamlined, and is constructed to make quick, short rushes rather than marathon-speed runs. Chain marks on the sides give the fish its name. Like all the pikes, the pickerel has an awesome mouth when looked at from close range.

Here's the standard technique to catch a pickerel through the ice: Go to the bait shop and purchase a couple dozen lively golden shiners that are 3 to 4 inches long. Drive to your favorite lake, and transport your equipment out onto the ice. Several good tip-ups should be included in the tackle list. If you're familiar with the lake, you'll know where the weed beds are. Cut holes right over the beds, preferably where the water is 6 to 10 feet deep. In most cases, this will be in an area about 30 to 50 yards away from the shore. Impale a lively minnow on each tip-up rig, and set the devices every 75 to 100 yards apart. Pickerel aren't school fish, so each tip-up will be working a spot by itself. If a pickerel is then taken on a tip-up, chances are good that another one will come by to attack a fresh minnow. If the underwater environment attracts one pickerel it will probably attract more. Pickerel move a bit under the ice, but not a great deal. It's a good idea to leave an inactive tip-up undisturbed for a couple of hours. Pickerel travel slowly; it might take them a long time to discover the bait.

Smart anglers should check the minnows constantly to make sure they're still lively, and haven't become fouled in the weeds. I like to look over my bait about every 30 minutes. Pickerel will ignore a baitfish that hangs lifeless on the hook.

Since pickerel are found in weedy areas, I prefer to fish my min-

Chain pickerel are favorites among Northeast fishermen. This one was taken on a tip-up in a New Jersey lake. Tip-up has been rebaited with a golden shiner, and its flag has been reset in cocked position to await a bite.

now just over the top of the vegetation. This might mean two or three feet off the actual lake bed if the weeds are a foot or two high. Suspending the bait over the weeds will allow it to be seen better by the quarry. It isn't as apt to become entangled, either.

Another good spot for pickerel is a partially submerged dead tree. I've caught plenty of fish by setting my tip-ups about 10 feet out from sunken branches. Beaver lodges are good pickerel spots; there is always lots of underwater debris and twigs next to the lodge.

It pays to know a lake before icefishing for pickerel. Many little hot spots are almost impossible to find when ice covers the lake. Practically every man-made lake has areas where underwater stumps are plentiful. These are great pickerel spots as are areas where rotted trees and logs are completely hidden.

More pickerel are lost because of impatient fishermen than any other reason. When a pickerel hits a minnow, he doesn't fool around. He makes a short lunge, clamps down on it hard between his jaws, and moves off to swallow it. Some people claim a pickerel will scale a minnow crosswise in its mouth before swallowing it. I don't believe this—I've watched plenty of pickerel in aquariums and under boat docks, and never observed them scaling a fish.

A pickerel does need a bit of time to turn the minnow headfirst and get it going down his mouth. The fishermen who sets the hook before the bait is heading into the pickerel's belly will simply jerk the minnow out of the fish's mouth or will pull the hook loose, leaving the pickerel with a free meal.

To avoid this premature faux pas, I like to wait at least 60 seconds after I reach the tip-up before setting the hook. This delay usually results in a pretty good share of successful hook-ups. Some anglers like to wait until the line starts moving at a good rate, since this is supposed to indicate the bait has been swallowed. Either technique works with equal success.

Pickerel are so active under ice that in some areas, more of them are caught in winter than in summer. In a study of 28 New Jersey lakes, it was determined that icefishermen took substantially more pickerel than open-water anglers. Ice anglers were easily the most successful, followed by the spring, fall, and summer fishermen.

Although more pickerel were taken in the winter, it should be noted that more New Jersey anglers fish for pickerel through ice than in the open water. This factor obviously contributes to a higher catch rate in the winter. Nonetheless, pickerel are still cooperative through the top of a frozen lake.

A New Jersey Conservation Officer looks on as an angler displays a fine pickerel. This fish is one of the favorites in the state. Most are taken on a tip-up baited with a golden shiner. *Photo courtesy of New Jersey Division of Fish, Game & Shellfish.*

Northern Pike

The northern pike (*Esox lucius*) is as mean as he looks. His appearance is identical to the pickerel, but instead of chain markings, his sides are green with a covering of bean-shaped yellow spots. The northern is a much larger fish than the pickerel, and can attain sizes over 30 pounds.

This species is circumpolar, which means it's found in other continents besides North America. Big northern pike grow in Europe, and the British Isles contain some huge specimens. In fact, Irishmen claim they've eaten many pike bigger than the 46 pound, 2 ounce fish that holds the official world record. That fish was taken in New York's Sacandaga Reservoir in 1940.

In the United States, the northern pike ranges from New York west to the Dakotas; it's most prevalent in the Great Lakes. Transplanting efforts have resulted in new pike populations around the country, and many Western states now have fair numbers of this big predatory fish.

There are two attitudes that anglers have toward northern pike—they love 'em or hate 'em. The pike has a voracious appetite and attacks anything that moves; many are caught when they aren't

Helen Thielhelm plucks a northern pike out of New York's Saratoga Lake while her husband Bob handles the tip-up. Watching the operation with interest is Howard Dudley of Virginia, on his first icefishing trip.

wanted. Anglers trying to catch lake trout, arctic char, smallmouths, and walleye are often confounded by the constant harassment by eager and enthusiastic northerns. Pike (called snakes by those who do not love them) are commonly tossed up on shore for the raccoons and herons. This is unfortunate—northern pike are gamey sportfish on light tackle and are delicious eating.

The pike's popularity is increasing, though. In fact, it's fashionable to fish for northerns in some quarters, and icefishermen pursue them wherever they can.

Northerns are fast-growing fish. In the fertile lakes of southern Minnesota, a northern pike can grow from 12 to 18 inches during the first year. In the northern part of the state, they'll grow from 6 to 14 inches.

Pike are prolific; a big female can lay as many as 200,000 eggs. Young pike are just as vicious as adults. They quickly turn cannibalistic and eat unfortunate members of their own species. This may be a built-in natural mechanism to keep the populations thinned and uncrowded.

Like pickerel, northerns prefer weedy areas. Since the pike are often found in big waters, they'll be in deeper waters than pickerel.

Additionally, northerns are known to travel a bit under the ice on their constant search for food.

Some lakes have large expanses of weeds that cover vast areas. A good way to intercept a bedding pike is to place tip-ups along these weedy routes where pike are apt to pass.

Veteran ice anglers apply an interesting rule to northern pike: deep water—big fish; shallow water—little fish. Deep water is generally regarded as depths from 20 to 40 feet, and shallow water runs from 6 to 20 feet.

Many big pike are taken off points and peninsulas that drop steeply off into the water. These areas are often good ambush spots for forage fish. Big northern pike will almost always be found in areas that have plentiful food sources. Areas that attract chubs, suckers, and yellow perch will likewise attract big northerns.

Tip-up fishermen don't bother with little minnows for bait if they're trying to attract northern pike. Plenty of meat is the rule for pike, so four to seven-inch minnows get the nod as the number one bait. Big, golden shiners are an excellent choice of minnows, but they're tough to get in the winter. Suckers and chubs are good baits, and they have the added advantage of staying lively on the hook longer. Like the walleye, a big northern likes his prey lively and sassy.

The minnow should be fished just off bottom for northerns. If the underwater vegetation is extremely thick, however, it's best to raise the bait and fish it just over the weeds where it'll have a better chance of being seen.

There are very definite times of the day when northerns prefer to feed. The hours of 8 A.M. to 11 A.M. are usually the most productive, with a rest period between 11:30 A.M. to 1:30 P.M. Action starts to pick up again about 2 P.M. and continues to 4 P.M. In northern states and in Canada, where the days are longer, the best afternoon activity may be between 5 P.M. and 6 P.M.

Anglers often debate whether or not to use a wire leader when fishing for northerns. Some say it spooks the fish and inhibits the bait from moving freely, while others claim it's an absolute necessity due to the pike's needle-sharp teeth.

I used to prefer wire leader until the new heavy monofilaments for bass became available. Now I use a three-foot piece of 17-pound monofilament as my terminal leader. If a pike chews that in two, he's probably too big and mean to fit through my ice hole anyway!

Jigging is effective for northerns, but not nearly as popular as minnow fishing. Big, shiny lures are best for jigging; plenty of arm movement is necessary to keep the lure dancing. Hold tight to the jigging rod if a northern is handy, though. When he hits he'll likely smash the lure with a vicious, head-shaking attack.

A hooked pike is a mad pike, and a fisherman will have his hands full to coax the fish through the hole. Some anglers use a gaff as assistance in getting the pike from the lake to the top of the ice. The gaff is lowered into the hole before the fish is in view, with care taken not to let it interfere with the line. As the fish swirls under the hole, the gaffer makes a quick jab. If he's successful the gaffee is swung up through the hole and onto the ice. The forepart of the fish should be gaffed, if possible, to assist in guiding it lengthwise through the hole.

When one northern pike is caught in a particular hole, there's always an excellent chance for another. If the habitat under the hole attracted one it will probably attract more.

Muskellunge

The muskellunge (*Esox masquinongy*) is the king of the pikes. He is the champion—the supreme challenge of the north. The musky is known by more than 50 names in the United States and Canada. Whatever he's called, it's always with respect and reverence.

This fish, resembling at first glance an oversized northern pike, has a different coloration than northerns. Instead of white or yellowish spots, its sides are either barred, peppered with dark spots, or plain. The world-record musky is a 69 pound, 15 ounce fish taken on the New York side of the St. Lawrence River, in 1957.

Muskies come in one usual size—large. Directing one through an ice hole is a feat, and only the strong-hearted should be allowed to try.

Few icefishermen expect to catch a muskellunge. Most are surprises when they hit. Muskies never come easily through the ice, just as they are tough to get in open water. Catching one is always an event.

Anglers who try for the monsters through the ice do so with very heavy tackle, and very big baits. A 9 to 10-inch sucker is a good musky minnow, but it is often difficult to find in the winter.

Like pickerel and pike, muskellunge attack a minnow by grabbing it and holding it lengthwise in their jaws. Then they swim off a short way and stop, turning the minnow so it goes down head first. It is at this point that most muskies are lost. If the fisherman yanks too hard and the hooks are still outside the mouth, chances are good that he'll jerk the hooks free of the bait because of the musky's heavy weight.

The huge bait's size often requires several hooks. Trebles are often used, and many anglers like to harness a big sucker rather than actually pierce it with a hook. This keeps it alive longer.

I know a few icefishermen who try for muskies by setting one or two tip-ups with outsize baits over a likely musky area. This is usually over a steep dropoff adjacent to a weedy sand bar. Muskies often travel in lanes or migration routes, and evidence indicates they use these lanes all year. By fishing a bait in these areas, there's a chance that a musky might come by and spot the bait.

Muskies must usually be a minimum size before being kept. This restriction rules out using a gaff to assist in icing a fish. The reason is obvious—the gaff will almost certainly kill the fish; muskies that must be released will not survive. Even if the gaff injury is in the flesh, any wound that pierces the skin allows harmful bacteria to enter the body of the fish. Fungus infection and disease soon follows. Of course, legal muskies can be determined easily if the fish are big enough, so anglers may keep a gaff handy just in case. If there's any question at all, though, the fish should be landed as gently as possible. If it's sub-legal, it should be released immediately with a minimum of handling. Don't take time to take a photograph, either. Fish dry out quickly in very cold air and may suffer irreversible harm. If the musky has swallowed the bait, cut the line as far down the gullet as possible and let the stomach fluids dissolve the hook naturally.

Muskies are speared in some states where legal. More on this is included in the chapter "Unique Ice Fishing Methods."

The Black Basses

The black basses include the largemouth *(Micropterus salmoides)* and smallmouth *(Micropterus dolomieui).* There is little need to explain the popularity of these fish. The largemouth is unquestionably the most sought after fish in most of the country, and tournaments now draw professional fishermen who catch them for cash prizes.

Basses are still not terribly popular among ice anglers. Like my pet George, bass become lethargic in cold water and are reluctant to feed. Nonetheless, bass can be taken by fishermen who know where and how to fish for them. Perhaps the best bait is a 3 to 4-inch minnow fished just off bottom in 10 to 20 feet of water. Bass tend to frequent the same areas as bluegills. Artificial lures are not as productive because of a bass's unpredictable nature, but plenty have been taken on lures, jigs, and other assorted hardware. Many bass are taken in the evening by walleye fishermen.

Under-ice bass often go on feeding sprees. I've seen days when all we could catch was bass, and on other days we couldn't get one no matter what we did. There didn't appear to be any reason for this behavior.

Bass are illegal during the winter season in some states, so anglers must release them when taken accidentally. This could be another reason why bass are not commonly pursued by many anglers. Additionally, fishermen who feel that bass don't bite in the winter often won't take the time to go after them with the proper equipment.

A telltale clue of a bass under a tip-up is a long run after it takes the bait. Once a bass hits, it seldom stops but keeps on swimming

Don McQue shows a chunky largemouth black bass that hit a minnow. Bass aren't as active as other fish under the ice but are caught now and again. This fish was released because New York law prohibits the taking of bass in winter.

slowly, taking line steadily off the underwater reel. Bass don't mouth the bait like the pike, but usually ingest it on the initial attack. For that reason, bass aren't difficult to hook through the ice.

Whitefish & Cisco

These related species, both of the genus *Coregonus,* are denizens of our deepest, coolest lakes. There are about 10 species of whitefish and cisco, and their range runs throughout most of Canada and along the northern section of the United States. Ice anglers catch whitefish and ciscoes (called tullibees in some areas) by lowering small, baited jigs and lures in 40 to 60 feet of water. Cut bait made of sucker meat is a popular offering in many locales. Small minnows are the favorite bait on some lakes.

The best fishing period for these species is usually right at the edge of darkness. Dawn to 8 A.M., and again from 4 P.M. to dark is the preferred time to fish for whitefish and ciscoes.

In some areas, anglers chum heavily to attract whitefish and ciscoes under their holes. Canned corn and minced sucker meat brings fish in and keeps them interested while cut bait is lowered in the middle of the action.

These fish can grow to decent sizes (ciscoes 2 to 3 pounds, whitefish 5 to 10 pounds), so medium-size line is required, with 6 to 8-pound monofilament a good choice.

Whitefish and ciscoes are superb when smoked because of the texture of the flesh. The chapter on "Care of Your Fish" tells how to make these fish a table delight.

Burbot

The burbot (*Lota lota*) is the only member of the codfish family found in America's fresh water. It is a strange-looking creature with an elongated body resembling an eel. Also called ling, the burbot is nocturnal and lives in deep lakes. Most are taken by anglers fishing for walleyes and smelt. Burbot will eat almost anything. Anglers seeking them exclusively use minnows or cut bait.

Although burbots are good eating, many anglers find them repulsive and refuse to touch them, much less eat them.

Since burbots are not considered to be game fish in most waters, there is usually no limit or season on them. Anglers who like to fish for burbot can do so with little regulation.

A Michigan angler lands a lake trout on a light-action spinning rod. Lakers are fished just off bottom in deep water. *Photo courtesy of Michigan Travel Commission.*

This Western fisherman took his lake trout with the help of a paddleboard. This hand-held device is filled with copper line that gets the lure down into deep water. Paddleboards, which are familiar to trollers, are equally effective for icefishing.

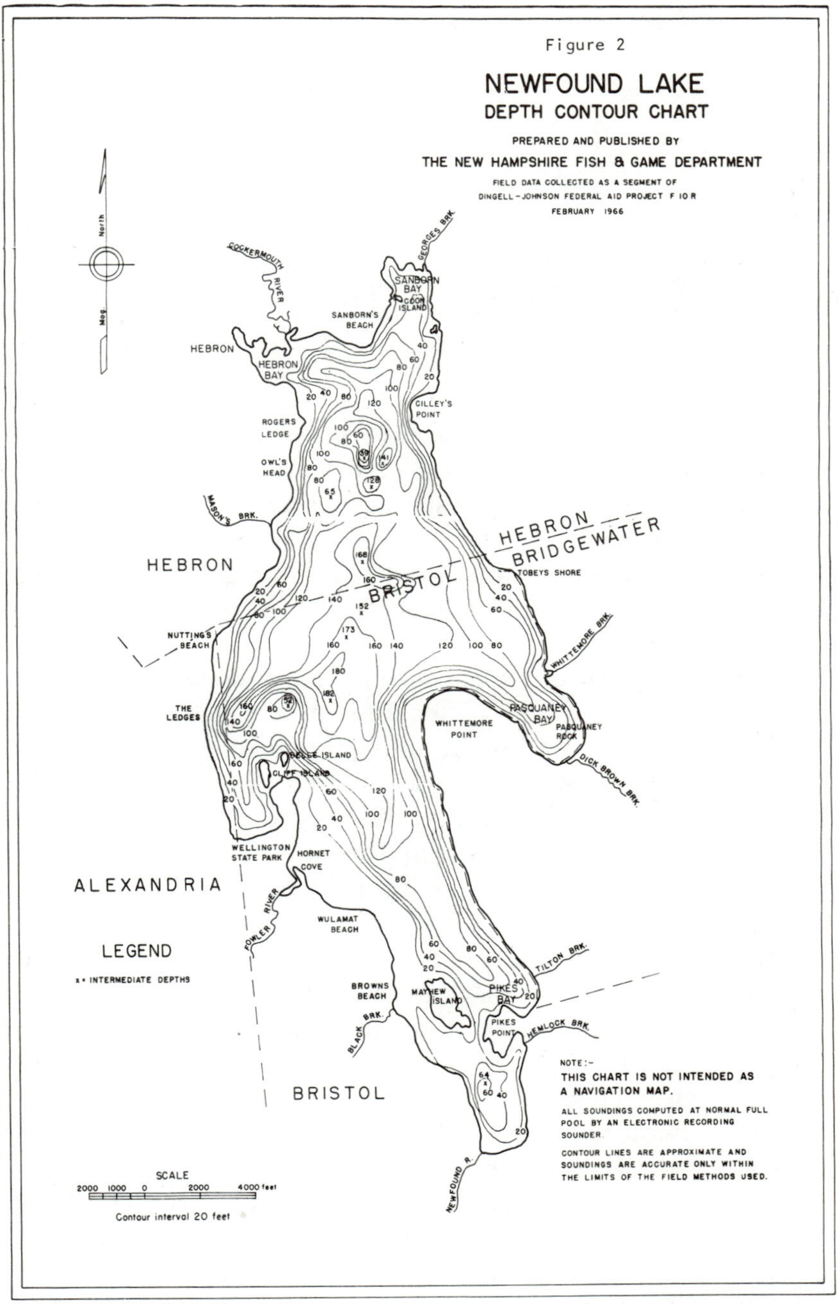

Depth-contour charts, available in many states, are of considerable help to you in determining depth of the water below the ice. Such information is especially helpful in states that have lake-trout fishing.

Cutting the Hole

One of my most precious possessions is the spud bar used by the men in my family for over 30 years. Passed down through the ranks, it ended up among my fishing gear when ice angling claimed most of my teen-age winters.

The bar was not purchased from a sporting goods store or mail order house. Like all ice chisels of those days, it was hand-crafted by a blacksmith.

Before the advent of the ice auger, great pride was taken by ice chisel owners; controversies often arose over whose was the best.

Practically every bar had an all-important thong attached to it. The thong was affixed to the chisel through a hole that was drilled near the top. The idea of the thong was to prevent the bar from being wrenched out of hands and falling through the freshly cut hole.

I can remember a balmy day during a New York winter when several dozen anglers quietly watched over their tip-ups.

The peace and tranquility of the afternoon was suddenly pierced by a stream of invectives that emanated from a group of fishermen several hundred yards away. A scuffle broke out among the group and a free-for-all quickly developed. A few moments later the men calmed down and resumed fishing. Spirits were lifted and friendships rekindled after a brown paper bag was passed around and its contents sampled by each member of the party.

We learned later that one of the men had lost his friend's 50-year-old spud bar because of carelessness. The chisel slipped through his hands because the thong wasn't wrapped around his wrist. Since the water was 50 feet deep where they were fishing, it appeared that the lake had claimed the chisel forever.

That incident was the only time I ever witnessed violence on the

These anglers team up to cut a hole efficiently. One uses an ice chisel (also called a spud bar) to chip through 28 inches of ice on Lake Champlain. The other fisherman follows each chipping session with a round of scooping out the broken ice with a ladle that has fine holes.

ice except when my buddy threw a frozen pickerel at me because I beat him to a tip-up. Thirteen year-old tempers flare easily, but the pickerel was not damaged. My pal apologized quickly when I failed to catch the fish on the tip-up.

The early 1960's marked a new era in icefishing. During that period, Swedish-made ice augers found their way to America. A rapid interest developed, and soon every avid ice angler owned an auger.

Tipper Hall of Highland Falls, N.Y., uses a spoon-type of auger to cut a hole. This style of tool is light in weight, takes down into sections, and is easily transported into remote areas. Here he's cutting through 18 inches of ice.

Augers come in different styles and feature a variety of bits. Most augers offer two popular sizes—6-inch and 8-inch bits. The smaller bit cuts an ideal hole for panfish and most trout, while the 8-inch bit is practical for northerns, walleyes, and lake trout.

Dull augers are frustrating to use, especially on thick ice. Bits may look sharp and feel sharp, but their performance will be poor unless they are razor sharp. Sharpening instructions usually come with most augers, but a lot of anglers prefer to have them done professionally.

The spoon-type bit is the most popular among modern icefishermen. The blade can be sharpened readily, and the bit fits snugly into a strapped-on protective sheath.

Despite good care, auger bits will eventually dull through normal use. In order to keep them in top shape, never allow children to play with them, especially on shore where there might be rocks and sand. Don't use the auger as a crutch to assist walking across slippery ice, and keep the protective sheath on it at all times when not in use. Never slide it to a buddy on the top of the ice, and be sure to dry it thoroughly after you get home to keep it from rusting.

The auger is very valuable because a single hole is seldom enough for most icefisherman. Since most states allow 5 tip-ups per angler, at least that many holes will need to be cut. Yellow-perch fishermen may cut 20 to 30 holes a day before they find a good school of fish.

The auger works on the same principle as the old-fashioned manual brace and bit. Hold the auger as vertical as possible over the spot where the hole is to be cut. Then apply pressure with one hand on the top while the other hand turns it. It's important to keep the shaft vertical and to maintain plenty of pressure on the top. A short person or child might gain more leverage by standing on a sled or box.

When the bit breaks through the bottom of the ice, water will quickly gush upward and fill the hole. Continue turning the bit until the hole is cut through completely.

Lakes along the northern part of the United States often freeze to unbelievable thicknesses. Twenty-four inches of ice is often child's play, and 30 to 36 inches may be just about average. Although manual augers normally have a reach of 36 to 42 inches, drilling through 2 1/2 feet of ice gets tough in a hurry.

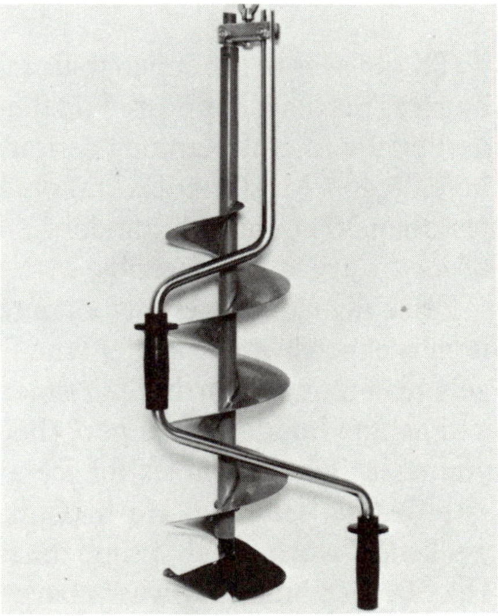

The drill-type of auger is becoming extremely popular throughout the icefishing states. This folding model can be easily stored in a snow sled or carried long distances. *Photo courtesy of Normark Corp.*

Power augers take most of the work out of cutting holes and are practical where ice is thick. Such a rig is of considerable help to fishermen who are seeking perch, bluegills, and crappies and must cut many holes to find them.

The answer to the super-thick ice dilemma is the gasoline-powered auger. This device appeared on the icefishing scene in the early 1960's and is now popular among serious ice anglers. It works like a post-hole digger. Most models run on a 2 1/2 or 3 hp engine, and weigh less then 30 pounds. A standard 8-inch bit can cut through 30 inches of ice in just a few seconds.

Price tags for power augers range from $125 to $175. Though the item is expensive, the angler who fishes a great deal on thick ice soon gets his money's worth. Sportsmen's clubs, lodges, family members, and fishing buddies often pool their money and buy one. I know one youngster who cut holes for ice anglers on Lake Champlain at the rate of 50¢ per hole. He had his power auger paid for after two weekends' work. At that time the ice on the lake was 31 inches thick. His 50¢ per hole rate was a bargain and a blessing.

Both power and manual ice augers can be purchased from sporting goods stores in regions where icefishing is popular. Mail order houses and large department stores stock them as well. Ice chisels are made commercially and are also available from mail order houses that carry fishing equipment.

If commercial ice chisels aren't available, they can be made by custom welders. It is important that the blade be made of quality steel that holds an edge well. The heavier the bar the better it cuts. A snow sled can be easily equipped to carry a heavy ice chisel to the fishing grounds.

I have a custom-made bar made out of one-inch pipe. The pipe was cut in half and threaded so both pieces can be screwed together when the chisel is ready for use. The bottom portion was filled with molten lead to add weight. A shaped piece of steel was welded to the bottom and serves as the cutting edge. A hole drilled in the top holds the important wrist thong. When broken down the bar is just 26 inches long and stows neatly in my ice sled.

An axe can be used to cut holes in the ice, but this tool does a sloppy job and scatters water and ice chunks in all directions. An axe can hardly cut effectively when the ice is much thicker than a foot. Even at that a huge hole is often the result because plenty of swinging

Neither a hatchet nor an ax is a satisfactory tool for cutting a hole through the ice. Chips fly in all directions, the hole can't be cut with even edges, and water is likely to be splashed on the person doing the chopping.

room is required. The bottom of an axe-cut hole is usually jagged and sharp. This is an undesirable situation and can easily fray a line and cause it to break when a fish is being played.

It is exceedingly important that the bottom of the hole be smooth and free of sharp edges. If using a chisel, cut the hole in the shape of an inverted funnel so the widest diameter is at the bottom. That way a fish has little chance of fraying the line.

A handy accessory that goes along with hole cutting is an ice ladle. This item scoops up ice chunks from the hole and keeps the hands dry.

Another welcome gadget is a set of ice creepers that strap onto the boots. Although all ice is slick, it becomes especially slippery when water flows across it at cold temperatures. This is inevitable when a fresh hole is cut. Tiny slivers of chipped ice and water from the hole make the surface treacherous. This is particularly true when there is no snow on the ice and the surface is slick to begin with.

It can be a real chore to keep a hole from icing up when the temperature is well below freezing. Some anglers pour vegetable oil or glycerin in the hole, but I don't like to add any pollution to a lake or pond. I don't want my fish to emerge through a slick, foreign surface when they're ready to be flopped onto the ice.

A popular method to keep the holes unfrozen is to float an empty can in the hole with some burning pieces of charcoal inside the can. The can is held upright by a piece of wire that is twisted around it or threaded through a hole punched in the top. The wire is then buried under a heavy chunk of ice or packed with snow alongside the hole. Unfortunately, the can takes up a great deal of room in the hole and is a nuisance.

Other devices are available to keep holes from freezing over, but most aren't worth the bother. Veteran ice anglers live with the problem and faithfully chip away newly formed ice as soon as it forms. The best way to keep holes open is to catch fish so fast that the hole doesn't have a chance to freeze!

If a large hole is cut for spearing or gigging, mark it well with branches or boards before leaving. I've seen holes in the middle of a lake that were large enough to accommodate a full-grown man. A tragedy could occur if a person unknowingly stepped on the thin ice a day or two later, particularly if snow dusted the hole and concealed it. Be sure to check state laws on hole dimensions. Some states wisely impose a maximum hole size for safety reasons.

Are fish spooked by the noises and vibrations caused by hole cutting? Some anglers agree that fish are indeed frightened; others claim that they're unaffected.

I had two experiences in different lakes that supported both schools of thought. On one occasion I laid flat down on the ice, covered my head with my dark blue jacket, and looked into the hole. Since the jacket blocked off the outside light, I was able to see clearly through eight feet of water to the bottom of the pond. I watched a school of yellow perch as they slowly finned around my motionless jig. I instructed my friend to cut a hole just three feet away from me so I could observe the fish. As soon as he started chopping with the spud bar, the fish darted a few feet away. They milled around nervously while the hole was being cut. When the bar finally punched through the ice they zipped away out of sight. Ten minutes later they were back to the jig.

On another occasion several friends and I were jigging for perch on a very shallow lake. One of my companions used a power auger and cut several dozen holes. Out of curiosity, I plunked my jig into a freshly cut hole while the water was still gurgling and surging about immediately after the auger was withdrawn. I began catching perch instantly, even before the water in the hole had a chance to settle down.

Although the incidents conflicted with each other, I suspect that most fish are spooked by loud unnatural noises. An exception might be a pond where there is a great deal of consistent human activity. That was the case on the lake where I caught fish in the freshly-cut holes.

TACKLE AND EQUIPMENT

A delightful aspect of icefishing is its simplicity. Since the quarry is directly underfoot, casting is never required. The offering is merely lowered into the hole and allowed to drop to the desired depth. Beginning ice anglers don't need to worry about expensive tackle. An attic, garage, or basement will probably supply all the gear required to catch fish under the ice. If tip-ups are to be used, they can be made quickly or purchased at reasonable rates from most sporting goods stores.

Many contraptions are often seen on ice, but few are really necessary. The idea is to stay warm, catch fish, and have fun. Those are the basic rules of icefishing followed by the millions of anglers who journey onto frozen lakes each winter.

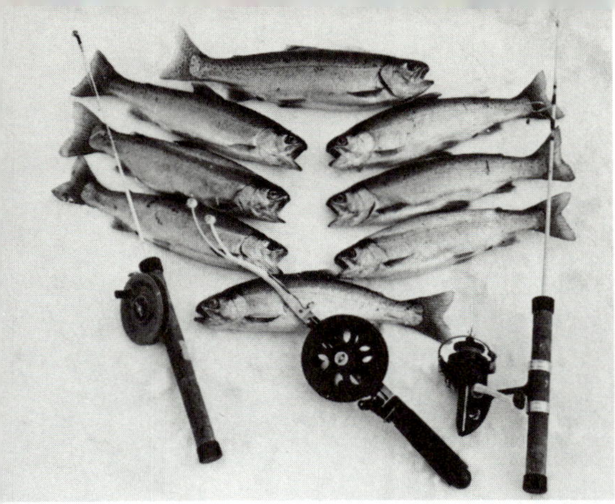

These Western rainbows were impartial toward the three popular types of jigging rods which were used to catch them. The fish went for ice flies, small spoons, and cheese.

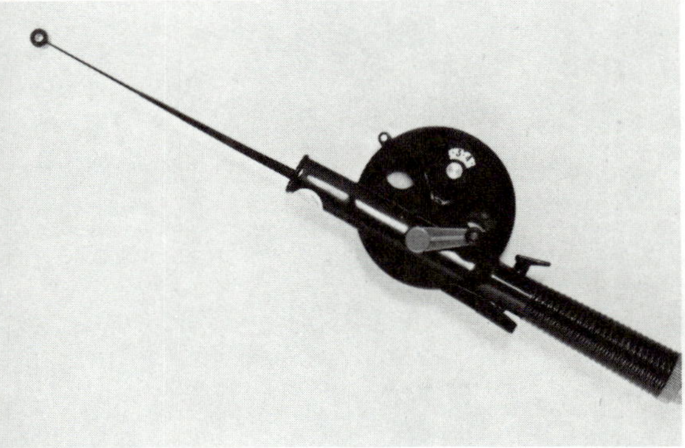

When you press a button on the handle of this special jigging rod, the tip vibrates. The slight vibration often coaxes fish to bite. *Photo courtesy of Normark Corp.*

Rods For Icefishing

Every type of angling has its specialized equipment, and icefishing is no exception. Modern-day bass fishermen wouldn't be caught without a stiff casting rod and a crank-type, level-wind casting reel. Dry-fly enthusiasts would be shunned by their peers if they showed up with anything less than a split-bamboo rod grown in Red China. The spin-fisherman *must* own a graphite stick.

Since an ice angler fishes close to his boots, the best rod is the shortest. The jigging pole fills the bill nicely for close-in fishing. It is especially handy in the close confines of a shanty.

Jig sticks can be made easily from old rods, or can be purchased from sporting goods stores or mail order houses. Commercial rods

Opposite: This well-equipped angler is ready for just about anything. His equipment includes a ladle, auger, lantern, container to sit on (which doubles as a carrier for fish and gear), bait, jigging rod, and suitable clothing. Note the piece of carpet for extra insulation between his feet and the ice. *Photo courtesy of Merritt Benson.*

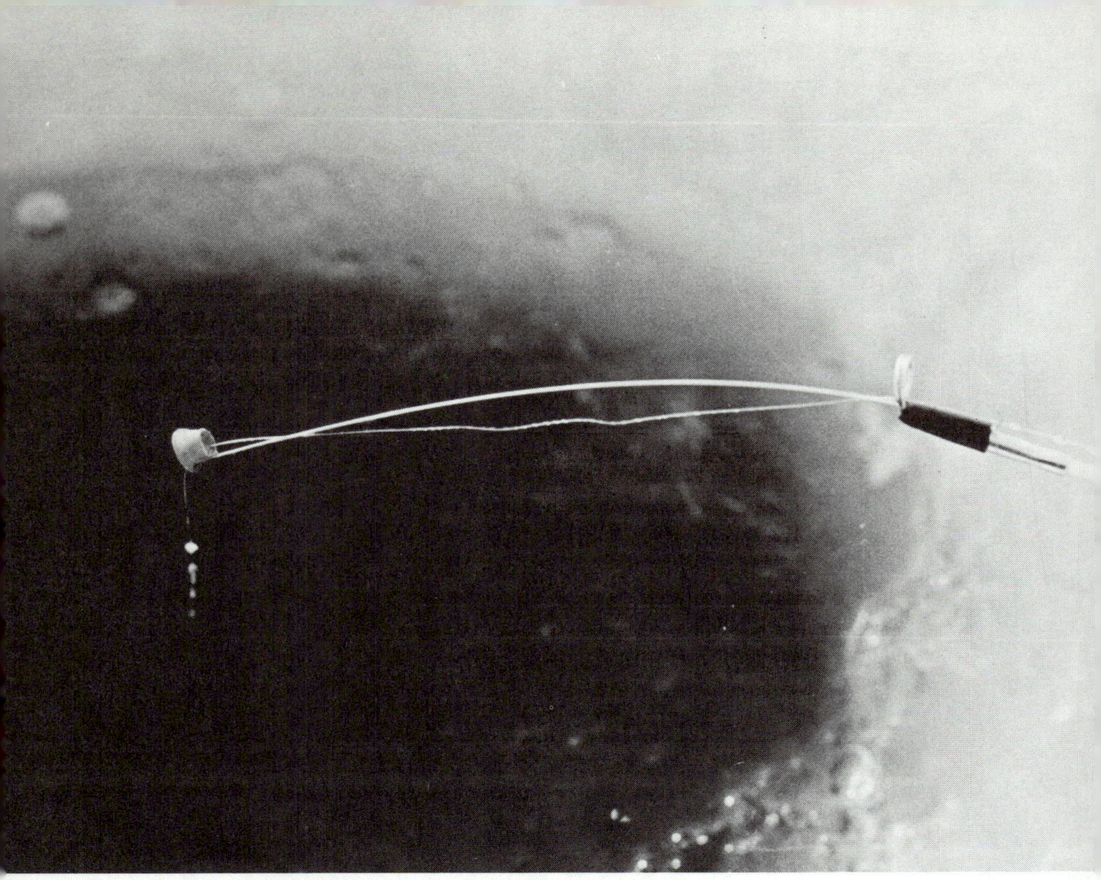

This extension tip helps you to detect sensitive nibbles and is helpful when you fish for shy species such as bluegills. The tip precludes the use of a bobber, so you can reel in the fish rather than haul it in by hand.

offer the ultimate in close-in fishing. One model is equipped with a button that causes the rod-tip to vibrate, adding a bit of action to the lure or bait.

Old rods can be converted into jig poles by simply cutting off the tip down to the first or second guide. This arrangement takes away some action, but the objective is still achieved. A better way is to cut the top 18 to 24 inches off an old rod and insert it into the handle. Of course, the rod section that fits into the handle must be evicted so the hollow of the handle can accept the rod tip. Any kind of strong glue will suffice to cement the rod tip firmly to the handle. When the reel, line and lure are attached, the homemade rod is ready.

A standard spinning rod will also work just fine. The big disadvantage is the necessity of standing several feet away from the hole, but this doesn't lessen the sport. The idea is to lower the offering into the hole and retrieve the bait or lure with a fiesty fish attached to it.

Whatever means it takes to accomplish this end is merely a technicality—provided, of course, that it's legal.

Some anglers disdain the use of a rod altogether and use a paddle board. This handy device is simply a hand-held piece of wood that quickly takes in great quantities of line by manipulating it up and down. Each time it is turned, 12 inches of line or so is added to it. The wrists are the energy source for this technique. Paddle boards are usually seen among fishermen where the under-ice quarry is small and numerous. Lake Champlain anglers like to use the board for smelt because little time is wasted in getting the fish from the water to the bucket.

As a last resort, an ice angler can use just a line and lure. A hand-line may be just the ticket for the angler who enjoys a more primitive fishing technique.

Whatever system you choose, remember that under-ice fish, particularly panfish, often bite delicately in the winter. The more sensitive your tackle, the easier it will be to detect a nibble. Remember that the alert angler will catch more fish than his buddy who expects the fish to hook themselves. Be on guard at all times, and stay with the tactics that get results.

The Line

Besides bait and lures, an ice angler's line also warrants most serious consideration. Icefishermen often underemphasize this important item. Since the fish below are a captive audience, they have plenty of time to carefully scrutinize the lure or bait. The line is always in a straight-down situation, and is easily seen by fish.

Select line that won't spook your quarry. Every fish species has its peculiar built-in wariness, and behavior habits often dictate feeding methods. Some fish eyeball the bait for a moment or two and then make a decision whether to take it or not. Other fish spot the bait and dash in quickly to attack it.

Lively baits usually attract fish naturally. Since the quarry can see and smell the bait, they lose much of their wariness. A minnow-baited rig, for example, presents an offering that sends natural vibrations through the water, and gives off a delicious scent. Large predatory fish seldom waste time looking over line and rigging if they're in the mood to pounce on a minnow. Six to eight-pound test monofilament line is suitable for fish like pickerel, walleyes, and largemouth bass. Heavier line is a good idea for larger fish such as northern pike, lake trout, and other species that approach the lunker category. Fish under ice apply a great deal of strain to line and tackle, since there is little opportunity to tire the fish with rod action. Hooked fish pull downward and thrash in all directions. Since the line will certainly be pressed tightly against the underside of the hole, there is a good possibility that sharp ice will weaken and even break it under strain.

Predatory fish are usually equipped with sharp teeth. Pickerel, pike, muskies, and walleyes all have fierce sets of choppers. When pursuing these species, it's a good idea to use a wire leader, especially when minnows are offered. Predatory fish usually swallow minnows easily, so their teeth have ready access to the line three or four inches above the hook. Innumerable fish have been lost after the line was sheared by their teeth.

Light lines are prescribed for panfish for two reasons. First, many warm-water panfish species have the habit of congregating near the bait and looking it over carefully. Heavy lines are apt to scare fish away. Some fish, such as yellow perch and bluegills, often bite very gently. Only the lightest lines are sensitive enough to transmit the vibrations of fish that mouth the bait tenderly. For this reason, transparent monofilament in the two-pound test category is popular with panfishermen. Four-pound test line is the next best choice.

Weights and Floats

Larger lures and baits are heavy enough to sink easily, but lighter ones require weights. Split shots or wrap-around weights will take most offerings to the desired depth. The weights are most effective if positioned 12 to 18 inches above the lure, although some anglers prefer attaching the weights below the bait. Small bell sinkers are ideal for the latter rigging.

Keep weights to a minimum and use only as many as is necessary. Excess weight makes the rigging cumbersome and awkward and could keep fish at a distance. Too much weight also eliminates much of the hand-line sensitivity required for panfish.

A bobber is a nifty item to help detect light nibbles. This is the main reason for using a float when icefishing, since it's easy to maintain the desired depth without one. The clip-on, plastic, red-and-white bobber is handy since it can be quickly attached or taken

Before fishing for crappies in a Western lake, Wayne Nicolls attaches a weight to the end of his line with a simple spring clamp. The weight goes quickly to the bottom, and he can see how deep the water is.

off the line. Another type is the sponge-rubber bobber that may be the most sensitive of all. An advantage of this bobber is the fact that it can be squeezed or even stepped on when it ices up, and then can be put back to use immediately.

A float can make a big difference. On one occasion I fished for rainbow trout on a Colorado lake with two companions. I used a bobber and they didn't. We fished with soft yellow cheese just off the bottom in 30 feet of water. It became apparent that the trout were teasing our baits with subtle nibbles. My bobber danced merrily on the surface of my ice hole but refused to go under. I watched intently, and, by trial and error, learned when to strike by watching the bobber movements. I landed four trout in an hour, but my partners, together, had taken only one fish. When they clipped bobbers to their lines they began to score immediately. That experience taught us that a float telegraphs tiny messages that can be translated quickly enough to enable the angler to set the hook at the right time.

The Tip-Up

Most icefishing equipment is interchangeable and can be used during other seasons. The tip-up, however, is strictly an ice angler's tool, and may be the official symbol of icefishing east of the Rockies.

Known also as "tilt" and "trap," the tip-up is a dandy device that allows an angler to set a bait that need not be tended. The tip-up is constructed so that a signal alerts the angler when a fish accepts the bait. A red flag is the usual signal on most tip-up devices.

The common tip-up consists of a pair of wooden support braces that hold the unit on the ice, directly over the hole. A vertical mast with a reel on the bottom is attached to the support braces. The mast is long enough so that the reel is totally submerged under the water. A wire with a flag on the end is attached to the top of the mast. When the tip-up is prepared for action, the flag is bent over and set so that it will spring up when the reel is turned. A striking fish will warn the angler with a "flag up."

The strategy of tip-up fishing depends on a fish holding onto the bait long enough for the angler to dash over and set the hook. This game plan works nicely with minnows, because predator fish are apt to grab a minnow and dash off with it in their mouths. More often than not a fisherman arrives at the waving flag to see the underwater reel slowly unwinding. If he's on the ball he'll set the hook firmly and retrieve his reluctant quarry hand over hand. If not he rebaits and tries again.

Heavy-green cotton line of at least 25-pound test is commonly used on tip-ups, although any kind of line will suffice. Coated fly lines have recently become popular on the icefishing scene. Some anglers prefer to use 6 to 10-pound test monofilament on underwater reels.

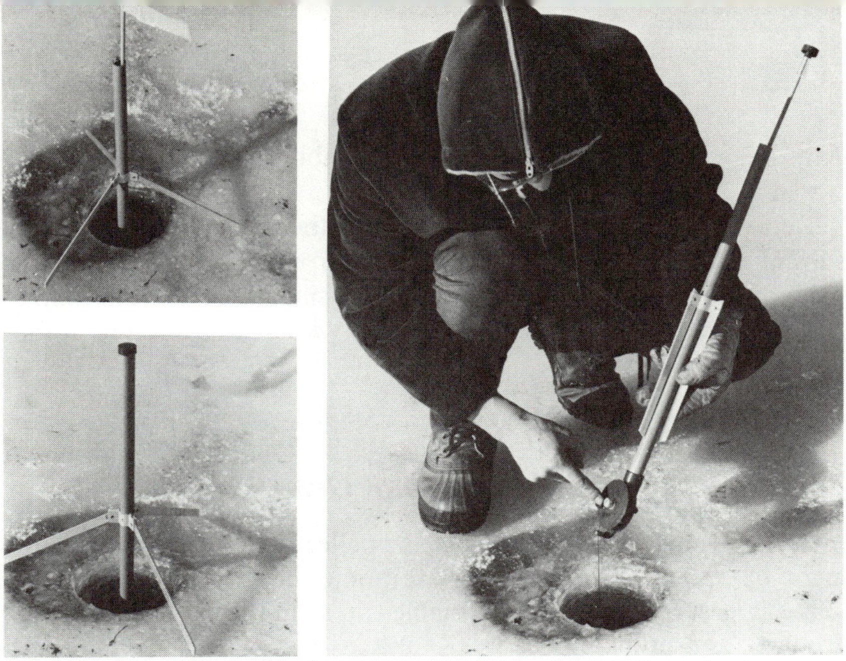

When a fish strikes the bait at the end of this tip-up's line, the flag pops up out of the cylinder. *Photo courtesy of The Worth Company.*

Same tip-up is shown here in cutaway view and close-ups of how it works. The device folds into a compact unit for carrying and storage. *Photo courtesy of The Worth Company.*

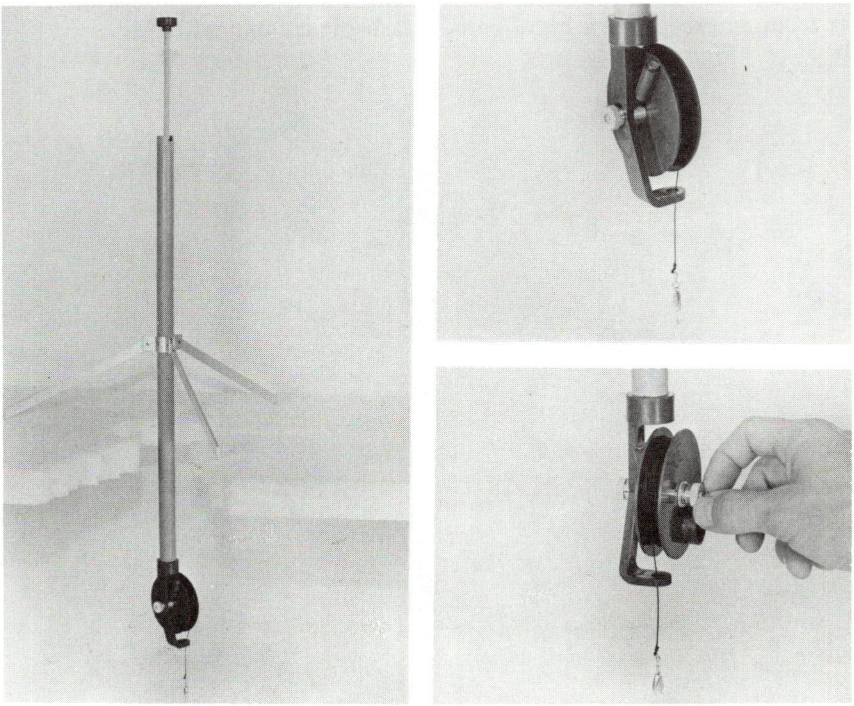

Any line selected should remain reasonably flexible in very cold water.

Remember to respect all members of the pike family for their substantial teeth. Hooks that range in size from No. 3 to 2/0 are ideal for largemouth bass, while 2/0 to 6/0 are suitable for northern pike and muskies. Details on hook sizes and types will be covered in the chapter on natural baits.

Moving Your Gear

It's one thing to amass a handsome collection of icefishing equipment, but quite another to transport it onto the ice. Most ice anglers make at least one very uncomfortable trip from the car to the fishing grounds, and probably two.

This tough task can be eliminated by rigging up a child's snow sled to carry your tackle. This handy item can be quickly prepared in five minutes. It can also be an elaborate vehicle with perfectly sized compartments that neatly hold every item in a special place.

Jerry Horgesheimer hauls his gear onto a Western lake aboard an ordinary sled made for a child. No special construction or preparation is required except for a bit of cord to lash the equipment tight.

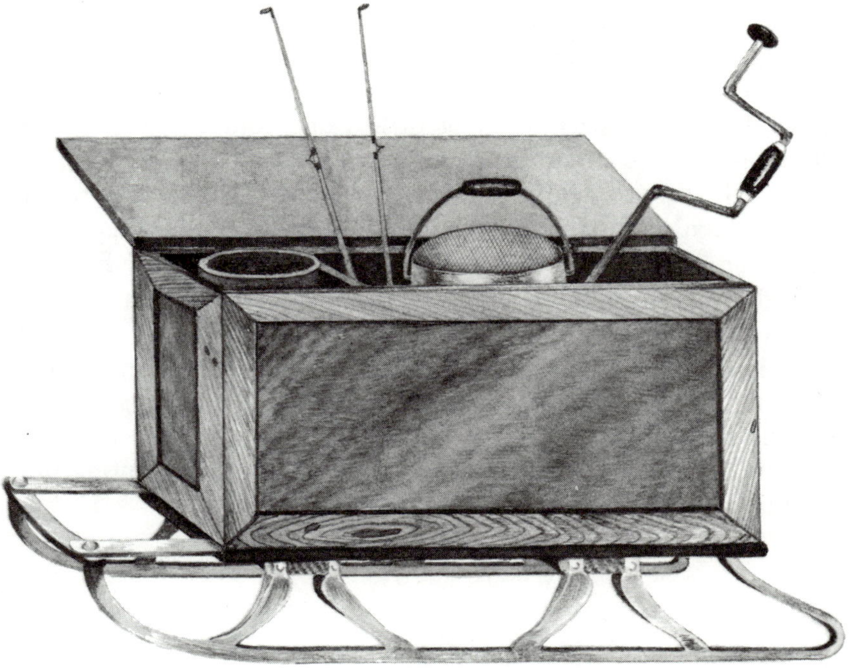

A more elaborate arrangement is this "customized" sled complete with carrying box and compartments.

The fastest way to construct a tackle sled is to bolt a wooden box on top of a discarded sled. Another possibility is to fasten a pair of cast-off skis to the bottom of a box. A pull rope is then attached to the front end. The do-it-yourself handyman can come up with all sorts of variations and can turn out a practical sled with just a bit of ingenuity, nails, and plywood.

Another way to transport equipment onto the ice is to strap on a trapper's pack-basket. The baskets are roomy and have the capacity to hold plenty of gear.

Assorted Tackle Items

Anglers who use minnows will remember their bait pails but might forget a small dipnet. This isn't an essential item, but it saves wear and tear on the fingers in frigid weather. Immersing an unprotected hand into the bait bucket to catch a minnow is not a comfortable experience, especially on a windy, bitter-cold day. If dipnets can't be found in sporting goods stores, try the local pet shop where tropical fish are sold.

A seat makes life easier between bites. Many anglers sit on their snow sleds. Others carry along little camp folding stools. Light aluminum lawn chairs do the job, but are a bit bulky.

A small stove or heater could be a blessing if the temperature is cold. Catalytic units used in camping are ideal. Besides using the stoves for heat, they can be used for frying a hot lunch. Freshly-cooked hot dogs and hamburgers are a tasty treat, and provide a bit of diversion.

An ice ladle is a great tool to scoop the ice chips out of the hole. Like the minnow dipnet, it keeps your hands and fingers out of freezing water.

There are numerous other gadgets that make an ice outing fun, comfortable, and successful.

Artificial Lures

As late as 1950, few anglers knew about lures that could take fish below the ice. Most anglers believed that fish wouldn't strike anything other than a minnow during the winter season. When I was a youngster, yellow perch and pickerel were the sole quarry. My pals and I had no idea that bluegills, crappies, and other fish could be caught through ice. We thought that most fish "hibernated," so to speak, and simply would not feed.

A look at the evolution of modern fishing reveals profound changes in lures and techniques. Consider the invention of the plastic worm and its tremendous impact on bass fishing. Icefishing witnessed a similar boom when small lures were designed exclusively for fishing below the ice. These lures were initially made with only one or two designs, but innovative manufacturers and individual fishermen began creating new models. Today, hundreds of excellent icefishing lures are being used by anglers nationwide. Undoubtedly, many more will be designed in the future.

Every artificial lure must be kept moving to attract a fish, especially when fishing through the ice. An angler who casts a lure into open water can vary his retrieve any way he wishes. The ice fisherman has little flexibility when his lure dangles on a straight line directly below the ice hole.

The only answer is to move the lure up and down. There are innumerable ways to accomplish this, but here are the most-common motions:

Jig And Stop. When using this method, the angler jerks the rod up sharply and lowers it immediately. After a pause of 5 to 20 seconds, the motion is repeated. This technique causes the lure to lift

Left: These jigging lures are designed to remain horizontal in the water. They're becoming popular among ice anglers, especially those seeking big quarry such as lake trout, walleyes, and pike. *Photo courtesy of Normark Corp.*

Right: Shown here in two sizes, this popular jigging lure is effective on most fish. Many anglers sweeten the hook by impaling a strip of sucker or other meaty bait. *Photo courtesy of Normark Corp.*

up quickly in the water and flutter down again where it rests quietly until the next upward pull.

Constant Jig. This technique always keeps the lure dancing and fluttering. The rod is constantly lifted and lowered with no hesitation. The lure is always moving, and is usually raised and lowered 10 to 18 inches as it flutters about.

Long Sweep. The rod is steadily raised upward and lowered slowly enough so the lure is always on a tight line. The lure doesn't flutter wildly on the down swing, but is controlled by the line, which has no slack. This is especially useful for yellow perch that like to wallop the lure on the way down. Since the line is tight, the strike can be easily felt.

The Twitch. This tactic is used for small lures and ice flies that work best when they're just barely wiggled. Some fish, like bluegills, are shy in winter and are easily scared off by flashing, quick-moving lures. The twitch, with its slight, tantalizing motion, helps them make up their minds. This method is accomplished by barely snapping the rod tip. Some rods are specially designed with a little button that causes the tip to vibrate. One of these devices is called a thrumming rod.

Most anglers combine jigging methods, until they find one that produces fish. Different fish species prefer certain jigging movements and motions. Each lure is most effective with a particular technique. The best way to find the superior method is to test them all. If that doesn't work, try asking a successful fisherman. Many times an angler with an unusually large number of fish around his hole is doing something that nobody else is. His jigging technique might be the key.

Lures may be sweetened with a meaty bait. In the case of panfish, the majority of anglers use some kind of bait with their lure to attract fish. This is often necessary since fish are even more wary under ice. They lose their shyness when they can smell an inviting scent on a lure.

Some ice anglers refuse to fish with a "tainted" lure. Most fly fishermen, for example, will go home emptyhanded from a trout stream rather than use worms. These "purists," are proud of their ability to catch fish on a piece of steel, copper, rubber, or feather. It's unquestionably more difficult to entice fish under the ice without the aid of bait.

The Russian hooks that made their debut in the Lake States were the first lures designed to catch panfish under the ice. They're small copper or brass spoon-type lures with just a single hook attached to the rear end. The single hook is significant, it allows for the addition of a bait.

Any book on icefishing is not complete if it doesn't mention the Swedish Pimple. This lure is a heavy slender spoon fitted with a treble hook. It has revolutionized icefishing, throughout the country, especially in California and other Western states, where icefishing was late getting started. The Pimple works well with or without a bait. It comes in assorted sizes and will take bluegills as well as lake trout. Millions of Pimples are used during each winter season.

Larger spoons of various colors and shapes are especially manufactured for icefishing. These are made by Mepps, Worth, Normark, and other companies. All these lures have one thing in common—they flash and shine. This is a necessary requirement for a lure that is usually worked in dark water.

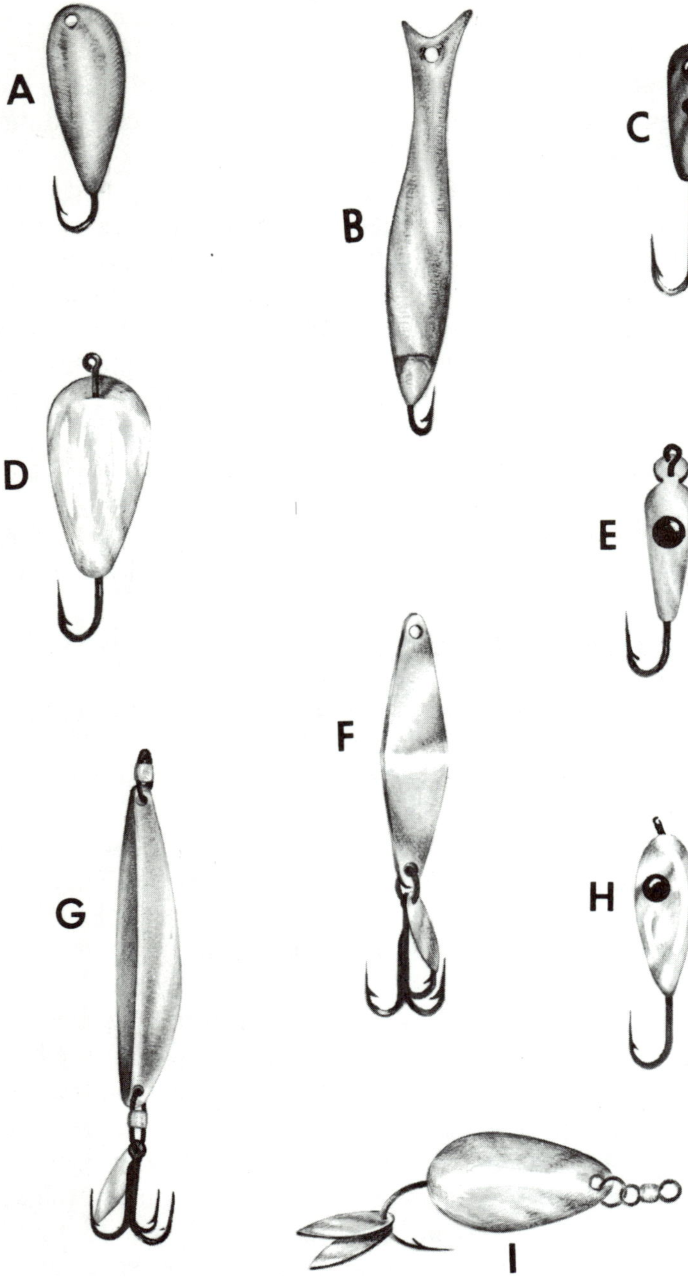

Key to identifying the lures: A—New Russian Hook, B—The Russian Hook; C—Dinner Plate, D—Mitzi Spoon, E—The Killer Jig, F—The Do-Jigger, G—The Swedish Pimple, H—Tear-Drop Jig, I—Flicker. *Courtesy of Dickey Tackle Company.*

The tiny tear-drop jigs have been longtime favorites among icefishermen. These lures (shaped like a tear-drop) are excellent for panfish. Some are outfitted with colorful plastic pieces that flutter and make the lure appear more lifelike. Tear-drop jigs are usually small—two or three may fit on a thumbnail. Many anglers carry only a handful of these tiny jigs, claiming that if the fish won't hit tear-drops they won't hit anything.

Some lures are used only as attractors. They serve only to arouse and entice fish under the ice hole, where a smaller lure is waiting. The attractor is jigged up and down vigorously, sending out vibration waves that attract fish. I know some Western lake trout fishermen who wouldn't think of fishing without an attractor to keep fish interested.

Ice flies are dainty little lures that are made to sink fast and catch fish. They do both. These lures come in lots of designs, shapes and colors. This lure can be tampered with on the workshop bench. An innovative angler can create anything he wants, and most of it will probably work under the ice. The ice fly is basically a split shot, clamped on a size 8 to 14 hook. Marabou feathers, rubber legs, a bit of floss or chenille, and some thread is all that's required to make the flies. Anglers not inclined to make their own can find all they want in sporting goods stores and tackle catalogs.

Three ice flies.

One of the most popular lures for Western trout is a marabou jig. This is simply a hook with a lead head and a marabou feather tied behind it. When the lure is jigged, the marabou undulates and shimmies with a delicious motion that trout love. To give this lure the action it needs, slowly raise and lower the rod tip about eight inches. The jig will climb and fall, and it resembles a shrimp swimming through the water. These jigs usually come in 1/8, 1/16, and 1/32-ounce weights. The 1/16 seems to work best. Crappies will also hit these jigs, with or without bait.

Larger jigs are used for bigger fish, especially walleyes. Some are fitted with streamer hackles or bucktail instead of marabou.

Lure colors are important to icefishing. This is yet another way to vary the offering. Some anglers are flexible about colors, but others are sold only on certain ones. This is not unusual; all fishermen form allegiances of some kind, even though common sense dictates otherwise. Fluorescent lures can work exceptionally well when other colors fail. Orange and red are the top fluorescent colors, and seem to work best on panfish. When I observed old timers using Russian Hooks that they'd manufactured themselves, I never saw a lure that didn't have a spot of red on it. According to them, this was essential to attract fish, and I never doubted their word because they always had plenty of fish on the ice.

Whatever kind of lure you select, remember that it *must* be moved about in a manner that the fish find attractive, especially when no sweetener is attached. Throughout this book it's been mentioned that icefishing leaves little room for innovation. This is certainly true, and the success of the outing depends on what's down there on the end of the line. If you aren't using the right lure or technique, you're wasting your time. The fish ultimately decide what they want. It's up to you to find out.

A weighted jig for icefishing.

Natural and Artificial Baits

Any discussion on baits should begin with worms. After all, worms are synonymous with fishing. The sport's classic scene is a barefoot boy strolling down a path with a cane pole in one hand and worms in the other.

Worms also make excellent icefishing baits. The only difference between open water and icefishing is the availability of worms, and the fact that they require different storage mediums and areas.

There are three kinds of worms used by anglers: nightcrawlers, garden worms, and red wigglers. Nightcrawlers are the most difficult to keep; they require cool temperatures at all times. It's almost impossible to obtain nightcrawlers in the winter because they burrow deep into the earth to escape the frost. Once in a while, a few can be gathered where heavy equipment is excavating frost-free soil. Obviously, machine operators aren't too fond of people standing around searching for worms, so this practice is limited. The best way to obtain nightcrawlers is to gather them in late summer and fall. Then they should be packed in commercial worm bedding or a homemade mixture of varied ingredients. I make an acceptable worm bedding by mixing equal parts of leaves, shredded newspaper (black and white—not color), clean rags, old burlap, and sod. After the materials are thoroughly mixed, they are slightly moistened. Don't let excess water pool in the bottom.

The best container for worms is a wooden box, well-nailed to prevent escape. Several small holes drilled in the bottom will drain any water that might accumulate.

Worms must be kept cool, but never allowed to freeze. This can be a problem in winter, and the obvious way to solve it is to use an old refrigerator that is big enough to accept the box. Worms can also be stored in a cool part of the basement or garage where the temperature stays around 45 to 50°.

Perhaps the best way to keep worms with a minimum amount of trouble is to store them in the small containers they are sold in. One or two dozen worms per container is about right. An old refrigerator will keep them fresh for months. If the lady of the house will allow it, the family refrigerator will work nicely, too.

Garden worms can be stored like nightcrawlers, and they aren't as difficult to obtain during winter. They're often found just under the surface of the ground, even where it is slightly frosted. Garden worms tend to concentrate within the root masses of lawn sod and large clumps of bunchgrass. They keep better than nightcrawlers; they are smaller and have higher tolerance to warmer temperatures. During warm winter days, they can sometimes be dug on the south side of buildings, where there is no snow on the ground.

Red wigglers, or manure worms, are hardy little creatures. They are currently a big hit with worm growers. These worms multiply rapidly and have a wide temperature tolerance. They fare well in compost piles, where they help reduce compost to fertilizer.

They literally thrive in piles of decaying leaves and vegetation. I find all I want in the middle of the winter by burrowing into a big pile of leaves. When I reach under the first layer I have no trouble gathering a handful. They're as lively in the winter as they are in the summer. I take only what I need for a day's fishing, and carefully put the leaves back in the pile the way I found them. There will always be a handy supply when I need them later on. Red wigglers are sold in practically every part of the country year-round. If rotting leaves aren't available for a personal source, the worms can be ordered from dozens of growers who advertise in outdoor magazines.

Red wigglers should also be kept in a cool place.

Impaling a worm on a hook may seem like a simple operation. If it's done incorrectly, though, the fish might refuse it altogether.

Under-ice fishing often prescribes many different worm presentations. For example, bits and pieces of worms are sometimes more effective than a whole worm. Of course, the size of the worm makes a big difference. Nightcrawlers, for example, should never be used whole unless big fish are the quarry. Largemouth bass and walleyes could be expected to hit a whole nightcrawler, but a bluegill or yellow perch will probably be scared off by it.

The best way to hook a small worm in one piece is to slip the point of the hook under the band or collar, which is located about one-

This is the proper hook-up if you're using a whole worm. For under-ice panfish, however, part of a worm often works better.

fourth way down from the worm's head. The hook point can either be left buried in the meat of the worm or pushed all the way through. When pieces of worm are used, the segment should cover the barb and curve of the hook. Enough of the end should be left dangling to give the fish a visible target.

The hook size depends on the fish. For panfish, I prefer a number 10 or 12. Bigger fish obviously require bigger hooks. The best technique to employ while using a worm is to lower it just off bottom. If the worm wiggles well and is lively, it can be fished "dead," with a small bobber keeping it at the proper depth.

Worms make great sweeteners for lures. I've had extra good luck using one on a leadheaded jig, while fishing for rainbow trout. They work nicely for perch and bluegills too, especially when impaled on a tear drop jig or Swedish Pimple.

Minnows

Since icefishing is a straight up and down situation, minnows are effective bait because they swim and act naturally. All other lures and baits must be lowered on a straight line and mechanically jigged and danced around.

Minnows are also good winter baits because they're easy to obtain. Thousands of people make a living selling minnows to ice fishermen. Although I buy my share of minnows, I enjoy catching my own. Many folks aren't aware that minnows can be captured during winter when the usual sources are frozen over. In fact, it often works better than in open water.

The places that yield minnows in the summer will do likewise in the winter, although it's best to try for them in water a bit deeper.

Obviously, a 2-foot deep slough in the summer will have only 6 inches of water if the ice layer is 18 inches thick. A standard minnow trap won't fit between the ice and the bottom of the slough. Slow-moving streams are good sources of minnows, especially in deep holes where they tend to congregate in the winter. To catch my minnows, I use a wire minnow trap that has an inverted funnel at each end. The fish swim into the funnel and inside the body of the trap, and can't find their way out. A few chunks of bread attract the minnow to the trap.

If the source of minnows is located near other people, it's not a good idea to tie the trap to a stick or branch on the ice. It's too obvious and might be stolen. To solve this problem, fetch the trap out of the water with a long forked branch. If the water is muddy and you can't see the trap, tie a piece of light cord to the trap, and tie the cord to a branch which is jammed into the mud just beneath the hole.

Many times I'll catch more minnows than I can use. When that's the case, I put them in a specially designed holding cage that will hold several hundred minnows. The cage is handy to the traps so I can get to it easily.

There are many kinds of minnows used by icefishermen. Each species has different tolerances and characteristics, so it's an advantage to know something about the bait being used. There are almost 2,000 species of fish that belong in the minnow family; 192 are found in the United States. From the fisherman's viewpoint, minnows are broadly classified as shiners, dace, and chubs. Others that don't fit in these categories are simply classed as "minnows", a catch-all that includes any bait fish.

Shiners are among the most popular of the minnows for winter fishing. These fish are delicate, lively, and give off flashy colors. Some shiners are golden, and others are silver. Goldens are found throughout much of eastern and midwestern America and are preferred if they can be obtained. They suffer rapidly from oxygen depletion, but this problem usually occurs during summer. During the winter their respiration rates are much slower and they will live much longer in a minnow bucket. Other shiners besides the golden are the common, spottail, blacknose, emerald, and bridled. These fish are represented in most of the states. Golden shiners reach fairly good size, and may be up to a foot long in fertile water.

Chubs are tenacious, tough fish. These minnows are strong swimmers and head for weeds and debris whenever they can. On more than one occasion, a healthy chub has tripped a tip-up flag by its own power. Some of the chubs include the river, silver, lake, honeyhead, and creek chub. Chubs are sometimes mistaken for suckers because they have a similar appearance as well as a rounded body. A look at a chub's mouth, however, immediately identifies it. This large minnow may reach 11 to 12 inches.

Dace are fond of creeks and ponds, although some species are found in lakes. These minnows never reach large sizes, and are seldom more than three inches long. Dace are the least popular of the minnows used by icefishermen because they're the most difficult to obtain in the winter. Because of their small size, they make excellent bait for yellow perch and crappies.

Other common minnows are the fathead, bluntnose, and brassy minnow. These are small, hardy fish found in many Northern states, particularly the Great Lakes area. The fathead minnow in particular is a popular bait since it's usually plentiful wherever it's found and fairly tolerant to temperature changes.

These are some of the principle minnow species found throughout the country. There are many others, but they are too numerous to mention. Minnows should never be dumped into a lake when they're no longer needed. Too many waters have become contaminated with unwanted fish via the bait bucket. Stocking of lakes is a job for the biologist, not the recreationist who is only an occasional visitor to a lake.

Storage of minnows for long periods of time can be a bit tricky. Fungus infections and diseases can quickly wipe out a supply of seemingly healthy fish. Water that contains chlorine and fluorides can be lethal to minnows.

The best way to store minnows is to keep them in a natural water system, like the holding cage I kept under the ice.

For about eight years I kept my minnows alive in a spring that was dug out and lined with concrete by CCC workers during the Depression. The spring ran the same temperature year round, and the level never fluctuated more than an inch. The spring was hidden in a grove of hardwoods, and I took great pains to enter and exit it without leaving tracks or other signs. Unethical human marauders might have helped themselves to my hard-earned bait.

Many anglers don't have access to such areas; the next best thing is to keep bait in a cool place where they have a fresh water supply and plenty of oxygen. For temporary storage up to a week, minnows can be kept in a minnow bucket if air is allowed to circulate. An inexpensive aquarium aerator is a good way to keep oxygen bubbling through the water. Special tablets that aerate water are available at sporting goods stores, but must be checked constantly to ensure that a continuous supply of air is available. Minnows that are being kept for long periods of time can be protected from fungus with a chemical that is available in pet stores. Directions on the bottle indicate the correct application rate.

Some people will do anything to keep minnows. Once I knew a man who lived next to a creek. He diverted part of the stream through his basement. He had a perennial supply of fresh, well-oxygenated water and never had to worry about the health or welfare of his bait.

There are many various techniques of using minnows under the ice. Anglers who fish for crappies and yellow perch often use a bobber to keep the minnow at the assigned depth. Unfortunately, the fish must be retrieved by hand since the bobber stops at the rod tip and doesn't allow the line to be reeled in. Some anglers get around this by attaching the bobber in such a way so the line slides through it. Of course, this requires that the bobber be set at the correct depth each time a fish is caught. I'm a bobber fan; I prefer to bring in my fish by hand. I enjoy carefully working a fish to the ice and through the hole. Even though a bobber is used, don't hesitate to jiggle the minnow a bit. This movement might just be enough to attract fish that were uninterested or hadn't yet seen the minnow.

Sometimes minnows are hooked through both lips (top), but more often they're hooked behind the dorsal fin (above).

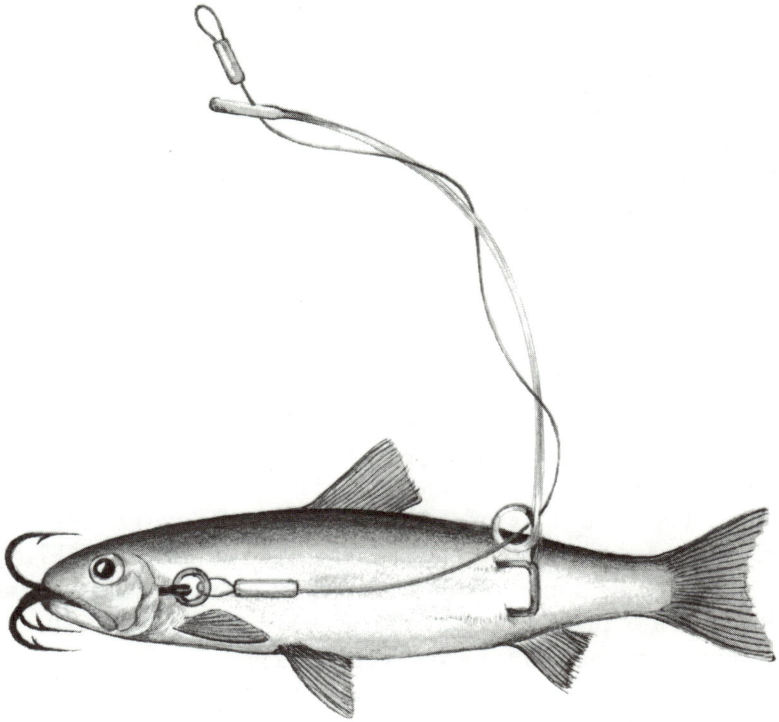

The Flagel bait rig keeps the minnow in a horizontal position. When a fish strikes and you set the hook on the run-out, the treble hook tears away from the bait and allows you to fight the fish in a relatively straight line on the nylon-coated wire leader. *Courtesy of Billy Boy Enterprises.*

Tip-ups, of course, go hand-in-hand with minnow baits. About 90 percent of all tip-ups used are rigged with minnows on the terminal end. Since the tip-up operation requires that a fish take a bait and keep it rather than nibble at it, the minnow fills the bill nicely. When a fish has its eye on a minnow, it wants to eat it. There isn't much nibbling around.

There are many ways to hook a minnow, but the most popular is to impale it through the flesh of the back behind the dorsal fin. Avoid puncturing the spine; the minnow will be unable to swim if its backbone is pierced. Another possibility is to hook the bait through both lips. This is sometimes preferred when fishing for pike, these fish normally mouth the bait and turn it head-first before swallowing it. With the hook in the mouth of the minnow, chances are better the quarry will be hooked if only the fore end of the bait is all that's swallowed. In all cases, a good healthy jerk is recommended to drive the hook into the bony mouth of a fish. Plenty of fish are lost because anglers are shy about setting the hook hard.

Some type of weight is usually required to get the minnow to the bottom, where the quarry is located. If allowed to swim free without a weight, a strong minnow may refuse to go down but swim just under the ice. A splitshot or two clamped about 18 inches above the minnow is the most popular weight. The weight shouldn't be heavy enough to spook a fish, but it should be substantial enough to keep the minnow down where it belongs.

Hook sizes and shapes vary with the bait used and species of fish being pursued. Snelled hooks are common, especially when heavy line is used on tip-ups. For crappies and yellow perch, hook sizes of No. 6 and No. 8 are ideal. Walleye, pickerel, bass, and northern pike are best fished with sizes 1 through 6, and muskies will require a 4/0 or better. There are some specialized hooks on the market designed especially for using minnows under the ice. One of these is the Flagel Bait Rig. It holds a minnow in a horizontal position, where it can be jigged in a natural fashion. Other rigs are available as well.

A common problem during very cold days is water freezing in the bait bucket. It doesn't take long to freeze water when the temperature is lower than zero. There is little one can do in this situation except keep the bucket in the warmest place possible. A warm shanty is the best bet, or the bucket can be kept in a vehicle that might be a few degrees warmer than the outside air. A fire on shore will keep the water warm, but it's inconvenient to run back and forth for bait. Most anglers chop through the ice in the bucket to get at a minnow and hope that they'll have all the fish they need before the bucket freezes solid.

For long-term fishing, an extra hole can be cut that's big enough to accommodate the minnow bucket. Then the bucket can be secured to something on the ice and lowered into the hole. It will never freeze this way. New insulated minnow buckets help to protect the fish during weather extremes but still don't prevent water from freezing inside the bucket when the temperature is bitter cold.

Minnows shouldn't be taken from a warm bucket and plunged into icy water, the temperature difference will be a severe shock that might kill them. To solve this problem, toss a small chunk of ice into the minnow bucket before cutting holes. By the time a bait is needed, the water temperature in the bucket will have slowly decreased, giving the minnows a chance to adjust.

Cut Bait

Cut bait is merely a strip of fish flesh used to catch other fish. It's so popular in many areas that it deserves a special mention in this chapter. Generally, cut bait is obtained from non game species such as suckers, carp, and burbot. Sucker meat is the most popular throughout the country. Suckers are usually caught in the spring when they're spawning and frozen whole until the following winter season.

The size of cut bait depends on the quarry, but most anglers use a strip two to three-inches long, 1/2-inch to one inch wide. The strip is usually impaled on a single hook by piercing it through the end. Jigging action allows the strip to undulate and shimmy about. Some anglers like to hook the cut bait to a big treble and fish it as they would a lure. In some areas this is a common lake-trout technique. Perhaps the most popular way to fish a cut bait is to use it as a sweetener on a spoon or large jig. When used this way it operates essentially as a pork rind.

Before considering cut baits for fishing, check your state's angling regulations. In some areas it is illegal to use the flesh of fish for bait, even though it's a nongame fish.

Larvae and Insect Baits

Every fresh-water fish eats some kind of insect larvae in its lifetime. This is the reason, perhaps, that these baits are so successful any season of the year. Ice anglers make good use of insect baits because fishing is vastly improved when they're offered, either alone or as an addition to a lure. There is a variety of baits available, and they're limited only by an angler's enthusiasm and energy. They can be obtained from nature, mail-order houses, and sporting goods stores, and there's virtually no reason why a fisherman can't find a source somewhere. This section of the chapter will tell how to get the most popular baits, as well as some baits you never thought of using for icefishing.

The mousee (also spelled mousie) is my favorite bait, as well as that of thousands of other ice anglers who like to catch panfish. It is the larvae form of the syrphus fly—a type of fruit fly. I'm not sure I've ever seen a syrphus fly, and I'm sure I've never seen a mousee other than in a plastic container filled with bedding. But this little

Among the most popular of all icefishing baits are mousee larvae. These extremely tough baits are the larval stage of the fruit fly. They can be bought at several mail-order houses, and sometimes several fish can be caught on one mousee. Drawing shows details of one mousee larva.

bait is perfect when I want a mess of bluegill fillets. The mousee is really a maggot with a one-inch, mouse-like tail, hence the name. Don't let the maggot affiliation turn you off, however. Mousees don't have a disagreeable odor, and when they come in a container they're just clean, little harmless creatures. These baits are sold in sporting goods stores and by commercial growers who advertise in outdoor magazines.

The mousee is at its best when hooked on a tear drop jig or a small Swedish Pimple. When the hook pierces the bait, it gives off a milky secretion that is supposed to drive fish wild. I believe this, judging by the evidence around ice holes wherever mousees are used! Some anglers use one mousee at a time; others prefer two or three. The baits have a tough hide and last for quite a while. Several fish can usually be caught on one mousee.

One year, mousees were almost impossible to obtain where they were commercially raised because of a natural disaster. A few anglers who had mousees suddenly earned many new friends, but the baits were rationed carefully. Lots of folks learned who their real friends were.

Mousees can be stored in a refrigerator or cool area. For best results, leave them in the container and bedding they originally came in.

Mousees catch all panfish species, but they are especially effective for bluegills. I've yet to see a better bait, particularly when bluegills are shy and biting very lightly.

Although I rate mousees at the top of the bait list, many others are quite effective. A variety of baits is always desirable because the fish below the ice hole may tire of seeing the same meat dish. This is a common problem in the winter when it's hard to vary your presentation and style.

Meal worms are good crappie baits and are easily obtainable from commercial dealers. If the sporting goods store doesn't have a supply, the local pet shop probably will—they're standard food for pet lizards, snakes, and other creatures. These baits are about an inch long, segmented, and have a hard yellowish hide. All panfish like them, and they're especially popular for yellow perch in some areas. The best bet is to buy them and store them in your refrigerator. A corn meal and sawdust mixture makes excellent bedding.

Goldenrod grubs are round, little larvae that spend most of their lives inside the stem of a goldenrod plant. Many panfish anglers refuse to use any other bait. In icefishing country it isn't strange to see grown-up people walking slowly through weedy fields, peering at plants. They're looking for goldenrod galls—the homes of the grubs. The galls are fleshy growths of plant tissue which feed and shelter the grub until it grows into adulthood—which in this case is an attractive brown fly. The most efficient way to gather grubs is to snip off the stem above and below the gall. Collect all the galls you want and take them home. Sit down at a table and gently slit the galls. If you're careful, a healthy, little white maggot will greet you from inside the gall. Place the maggots in a container that is half full of sawdust or commercial bedding. Store them in the refrigerator until it's time to go icefishing.

Corn borers are more difficult to find because their home isn't so obvious. Although they live in the pithy tissue of corn stalks, they must be located by spotting a tiny hole in a stalk remaining in the field. Energetic bait gatherers cut dozens of stalks and look for the borers later. Of course, you might need a farmer's permission to search through his stubble, and you might need a gun to protect yourself from the white-jacketed people who will want to take you to the local asylum. After all, not too many folks crawl around fields looking intently at frozen corn stalks in the middle of winter!

Wood grubs are the larvae of various beetles that spend their time in lovely galleries between the bark and wood of logs and fallen branches. These grubs are located by peeling bark off rotting tree parts. I have the best luck searching through oak logs, but every tree species harbors some type of grub under the bark.

Assorted grubs are often found in the material deposited by the wrong end of a cow. By winter, these droppings will be frozen and halfway acceptable, and an old hatchet might turn up some interesting creatures inside.

All the grubs and larvae mentioned so far are found on land. It's interesting that fish find them attractive because they're never part of their regular diet. That's one of the mysteries of fishing, though,

Wax worm (left) and wood grub can be effective icefishing baits.

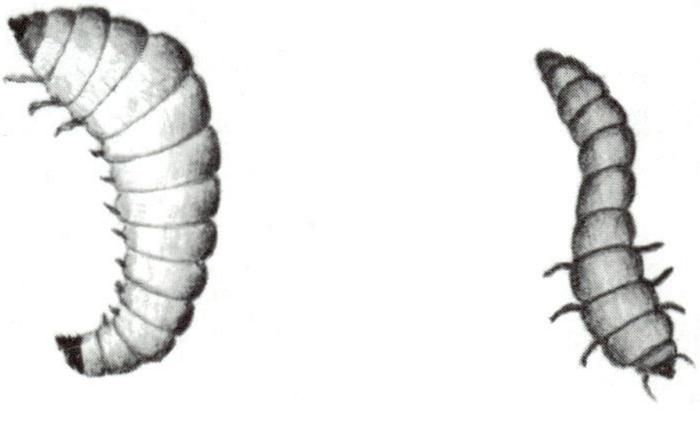

and it just points out the fact that fish don't think much before opening their mouths. The idea, then, is to give them something that is acceptable to their general appetite. They'll do the rest.

All kinds of larvae live under the rocks of streams and creeks, and many live in the mud at the bottom of a pond. They include the mayfly, caddisfly, stone fly, crane fly, dragonfly, and dobsonfly. Practically all of these baits can be obtained by turning over rocks and stones in shallow streams. In parts of the North, where bitter cold weather seals in running streams, it may be practically impossible to get at these baits. The answer is to gather them in late fall before the streams freeze over.

Why would anyone want to go through the trouble of gathering these baits when mousees and mealworms can be purchased in most stores? The answer is variety. As I've mentioned several times, anglers who score under the ice are those who keep the fish consistently interested in their offerings. Flexibility is the key, and an assortment of widely different baits is the answer to being flexible.

One of the best ways to gather larvae is to use a screen nailed between two wooden slats. The screen is placed upright on the downstream side of a riffle where there are several stones and gravels. A companion wades through the riffle and kicks over as many rocks as he can. Larvae will wash down with the current into the waiting screen. In small streams, individual stones can be overturned and the larvae beneath them captured by hand.

Caddisflies are common throughout the country, with over 800 species found in the United States and Canada. These insects spend their larval lives in a little shell that they carry on their backs. The shell, or case, is made of twigs, bits of leaves, and grains of sand, depending on the species. Caddisflies vary in length from 1/2 inch to over two inches. Since these larvae carry their protection with them, they commonly scurry over the stream bottom in full view. An alert angler can gather them by just catching them by hand.

Once, while trapping minnows in a stream during the winter, I was amazed to see the trap seething with huge caddisflies. I don't know why the larvae were attracted to the trap, but I continued to catch them throughout the winter. Either they entered the trap because it had bread crumbs or dead minnows in it, or they just wandered in because the funnels appeared to lead to protection inside. I wouldn't recommend spending much effort trying to catch caddisflies like this, but it might work again just as well.

Mayflies and stoneflies are much more shy than caddisflies, since

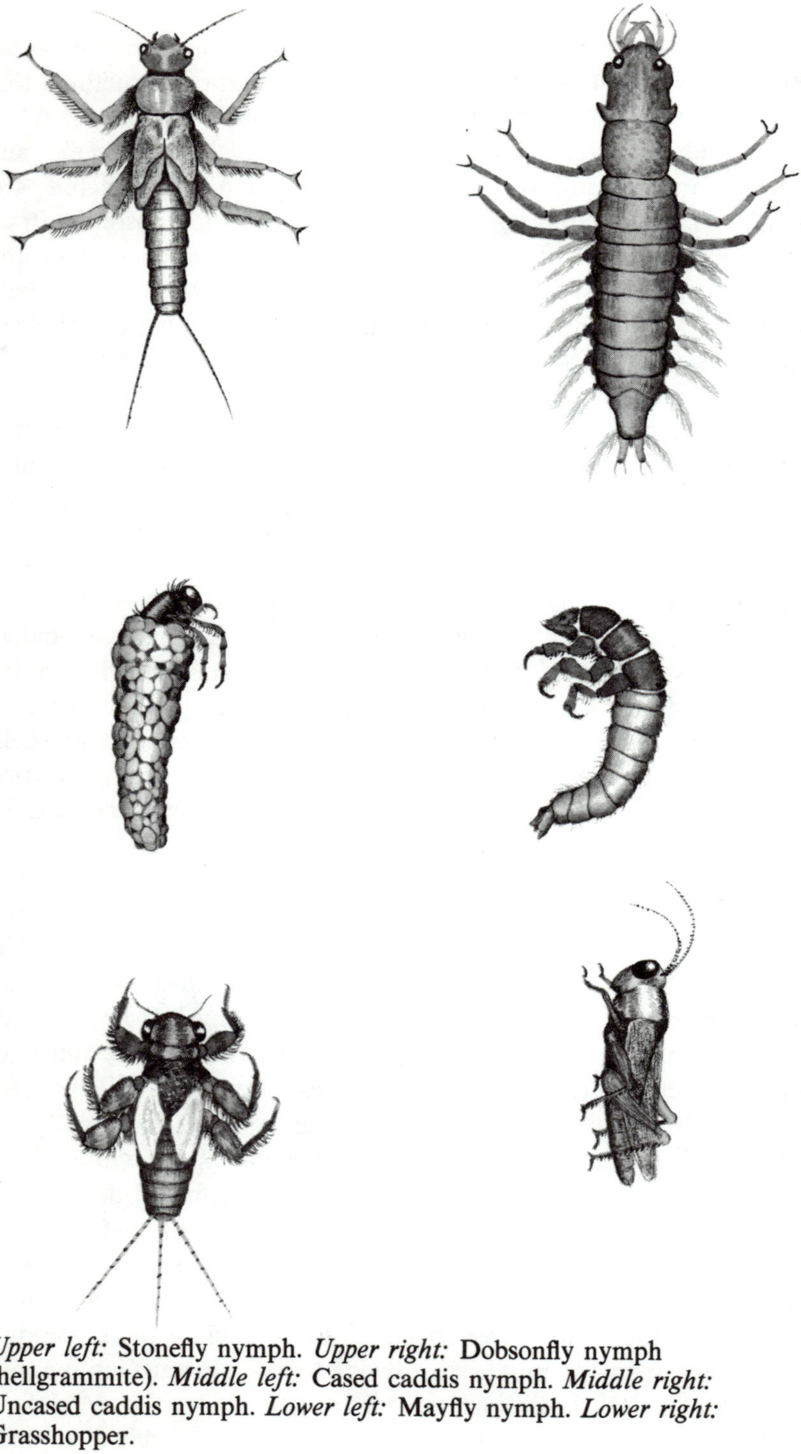

Upper left: Stonefly nymph. *Upper right:* Dobsonfly nymph (hellgrammite). *Middle left:* Cased caddis nymph. *Middle right:* Uncased caddis nymph. *Lower left:* Mayfly nymph. *Lower right:* Grasshopper.

their only protection is to hide under rocks and boulders. These larvae are eaten by practically everything that swims; they always make a welcome addition whenever they're offered beneath the ice. There are many species of these insects in North America with some 500 species of mayflies and 400 species of stoneflies.

The larvae of the dobsonfly is a scary creature known as the hellgrammite. This larvae possesses a pair of tusklike mandibles which are powerful enough to hurt a grown man if he carelessly allows himself to be pinched. The hellgrammite is best handled by holding it behind the collar where the pincers can't get at a finger. This larvae grows up to three inches long, and is practically indestructible on a hook. The hard, bony case keeps it well protected, and one bait may catch several dozen fish. Hellgrammites are a great find in many streams and in some areas it's a big treat to catch one. When I was a youngster we screened a small creek in southern New York that was known to support hellgrammites. The day was always a success if we caught a half dozen or more.

In the West, anything that crawls or slithers under stream rocks is called a hellgrammite. This is a misnomer, since mayflies, caddisflies, and stoneflies are erroneously included in that classification. Westerners catch winter larvae for use as whitefish bait in streams.

Dragonfly larvae might be expected to be huge animals because of the size of the adults, but they're really quite short and robust. These nymphs live under rocks and vegetation, and some species burrow in the mud of pond bottoms. I know a place where I can get all I need by excavating the bank of a pond where beaver have piled mud. A small shovel assists in the digging operation. The procedure is to spread the mud out carefully on the bank and watch for little things that start to wiggle around.

One bait that must be gathered during the summer and early fall and stored in the freezer until icefishing time is grasshoppers! This bait is no more unorthodox than a corn borer or piece of cheese, and may even strike a responsive chord to fish under the ice. Perhaps they recognize the insect from warmer days of the past. Grasshoppers are easily gathered in the late summer when the evenings are cool and dewy. The lethargic insects can be collected and frozen in a container of water so they're actually encased in ice. This prevents them from drying out.

The rest of this chapter will describe how to use other baits that aren't found outdoors in a natural state. They include salmon eggs, corn, marshmallows, and cheese. Most of these baits are used to catch trout, specifically rainbows. Panfish such as bluegills, crappies, and yellow perch are too selective to take this kind of bait, but rainbows are fond of these supermarket specials.

Cheese is the most common bait used to take trout in the West. It's quickly becoming recognized as such in the Midwest and East as anglers discover the merits of this bait.

Cheese fits in well with icefishing, and probably accounts for 75 percent of all rainbows taken in the winter. For years, Velveeta cheese was almost exclusively used for trout bait. It's soft and pliable, and easily worked on a hook. In recent years, however, other cheeses have been specifically manufactured for fishing. Today an angler can buy cheese spiked with anise, garlic, and other ingredients. As could be predicted, anglers now have favorite cheeses and swear by certain brands and varieties.

Special hooks have been designed to hold cheese firmly so it doesn't fall off. They are simply treble hooks with a small spring coiled around the shank. The coil holds the cheese intact.

The best way to apply cheese on a hook is to pinch off a small chunk and roll it between both palms until it forms a round ball. Then the ball is pushed firmly from the bottom of the treble so it barely covers the three points. As soon as the cheese hits the cold water it sets up and becomes firm. However, whenever a fish bites and the line is jerked, the cheese will almost surely fall off if the fish is missed. This isn't necessarily undesirable, though, because the cheese that falls off keeps the fish interested under the hole. It's really an unintentional form of chumming.

Single hooks are commonly used for cheese, and some anglers claim they have better success hooking fish with them. I've used both kind and see little difference in hooking performance. Treble sizes 8 to 12 are popular, and 8 to 10 are preferred for singles. A small split-shot is helpful in getting the cheese down quickly, especially where the water is deep. In shallow lakes, the natural action of the sinking cheese without a weight might elicit more trout bites, especially since fish can be found at different levels under the ice.

Salmon eggs are popular baits for trout wherever they are legal. Special salmon-egg hooks with an extra-wide curve allows several to be placed on a hook. Some anglers use trebles, and pierce an egg on each of the points. Like cheese, salmon eggs come in all brands, sizes, and colors. The best are those that "milk" in the water. After eggs are in the water for a while, they lose their color and fluids. That's when it's time to replace them.

Common canned corn is an excellent winter bait, and is frequently used to chum a hole. Salmon egg hooks are ideal for corn and are used by most anglers. There's some debate as to the ability of trout to digest corn. It's sometimes claimed that fish pass the corn through whole, and blockage of the intestinal tract can result. No solid evidence supports this possibility, but some states prohibit corn. One reason is the littering problem created by thoughtless anglers who discard empty corn cans.

Marshmallows are sometimes used for icefishing, especially in combination with another bait. Cheese-marshmallow combinations are locally popular in rainbow trout waters.

All of the supermarket-type baits contribute to littering because they come in jars, cans, or boxes. Always take pains to pick up after you're done fishing. There are few uglier sights than trash on the ice.

Ice Shanties and Shelters

Few scenes in the outdoors look as cozy as an ice shanty sitting on a frozen lake, with a spiral of smoke issuing from the chimney. A peek in the shanty will probably reveal an icefisherman sitting on a bench, concentrating on his line. A pot-bellied stove will glow red from the heat, and all the essentials for survival will be neatly stored.

Ice shanties, also called sheds, shacks, ice houses, shelters, coops and other names, are one of the reasons that icefishing enjoys the popularity that it does. Some folks are so fond of ice angling that a shanty is essential to protect them during the long hours they spend on frozen lakes. This is especially true in northern states and Canadian provinces. It's almost physically impossible to stand on the ice

Left: Interior view of warm shanty shows fishermen catching smelt on Lake Champlain. Temperature outside is 15° below zero F.

Right: Bob Thielhelm sets a tip-up outside a shanty on New York's Saratoga Lake. Window enables him to watch the tip-ups in comfort from the warm shelter.

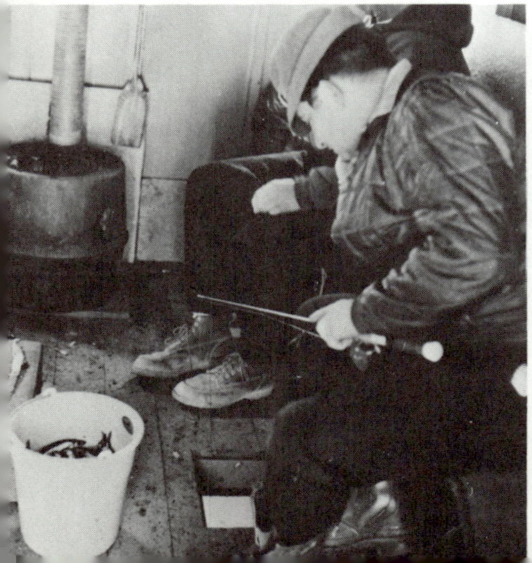

These shanties are on Houghton Lake, one of Michigan's most popular icefishing waters. *Photo courtesy of Michigan Travel Commission.*

when the wind howls and the air temperature plummets to 30° F. below zero. Although all kinds of clothing and devices are available to keep warm during adverse conditions, few people will withstand the punishment of a super-cold day. When frigid weather is common for several weeks in a row, some type of shelter is a must.

Shelters vary widely. Some are merely tents lashed to the ice; others are a few pieces of plywood hinged together to cut the wind. A few are deluxe models that contain all the comforts of home. Others are simply camp trailers or cab-over campers hauled out on the ice. It's not uncommon to see generators chugging away alongside a shelter, providing electricity for the appliances inside. Some lakes that attract thousands of shanty dwellers have electric service throughout the shanty towns.

While most shelters are simple wooden shanties that contain just the essentials, some are elaborate showcases that must be seen to be believed. I was invited into a shanty once that had a television, microwave oven, stereo, small library, and cots. It made one feel that he wasn't on top of a frozen lake at all, but in an elegant cabin or

Shanties dot this lake in Minnesota, a popular icefishing state. On some lakes, several thousand shanties have been counted. *Photo courtesy of Minnesota Dept. of Natural Resources.*

a beach house. The occupants of that shanty were a retired couple, and they actually lived in the structure for several weeks at a time.

The standard shelter is not that fancy, and basically features a stove or heater of some type, a bench or chair, perhaps a window, shelves for storage, a cooler with food in it, a lantern, extra lantern fuel, an ice-cutting tool, extra clothes, a portable toilet, and other items to ensure comfort and satisfaction. If the structure is big enough, a folding cot will allow overnighting.

New, portable canvas-type shanties are becoming more popular each year. These are generally pop-up units that fit over a tubular frame. The advantages are obvious: the shelters are mobile and can be moved at will. If the fish aren't biting in one area, only minimal effort is required to set up a few hundred yards away.

There are hundreds of shelter designs used by winter anglers. Icefishermen are an innovative lot; they'll improvise and fuss until they get the job done. In this case, the "job" is coming up with a brainchild that allows them to spend comfortable hours on the ice.

When you're in the process of selecting a portable shelter or building a shanty from scratch, visit an area where different shelters are being used before making a decision. Chat with the owners and ask questions. Experience is the mother of learning. Old-timers out on the ice can tell you almost everything you need to know. Consider your plans for fishing the same lake all winter. A wooden structure is probably too heavy to transport elsewhere; you'll be stuck with the initial location where it was originally set. As the winter progresses, snow may drift around it and pile high, making it difficult to move. If you decide on a wooden shanty, where will you store it in the off-season? Do you have room for it on your property, as well as a convenient means of transporting it? Can you rent storage space from a property owner on the lake shore?

This small shanty provides much protection on a cold, windy day. Because of its light weight, the shelter can be easily moved to a new location. *Photo courtesy of Ohio Dept. of Natural Resources.*

This shelter, which weighs less than 12 pounds, is easily assembled almost anywhere. It is sturdy and can be erected quickly by one person. *Courtesy of Dickey Tackle Company.*

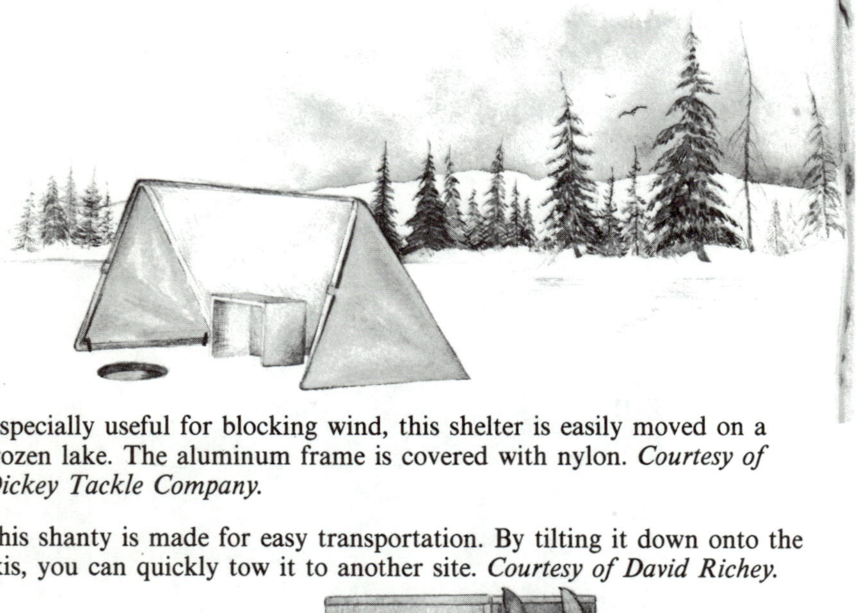

Especially useful for blocking wind, this shelter is easily moved on a frozen lake. The aluminum frame is covered with nylon. *Courtesy of Dickey Tackle Company.*

This shanty is made for easy transportation. By tilting it down onto the skis, you can quickly tow it to another site. *Courtesy of David Richey.*

Building a shanty is relatively easy. It amounts to nailing marine plywood on a wooden framework. The toughest part is hanging the door. Even if it sags a bit, no one will complain. If they do, banish them to the cold world outside your shanty! A window or two is preferred if tip-ups are used outside. Tar paper is a good liner to seal the structure and keep it waterproof. Remember to periodically shovel the snow off the roof.

Unfortunately, vandalism has spread to the outdoors, as well as city streets. In areas where there are large concentrations of people, especially during gala weekend events, it's wise to lock the door. On some Midwest lakes, over 10,000 shanties have been counted just over a few square miles.

Shelters have sanitary problems for obvious reasons. Humans must perform body functions daily, and this need should be recognized with some preparation before venturing onto the ice. There are many types of portable toilet disposal systems on the market. It doesn't matter what type is used—the important thing is that every shanty should have one. There are exceptions. Perhaps a nearby filling station or public building has toilet facilities within easy walking distance of the shelter. Portable outbuildings are sometimes hauled onto the ice during ice festivals and carnivals.

Shelter safety is important. Most shelters have some type of heat source to keep the occupants warm. First of all, place all flammable liquids and materials a safe distance away from open flames. *Always* keep in mind the fact that poisonous fumes are possible whenever combustion takes place. Whenever a substance is burning, oxygen is required to feed the combustion process. In a closed area as inside of a shelter, an oxygen deficit may occur because of the burning requirement.

As a result, combustion becomes inefficient, and incomplete burning may result. Carbon monoxide, a deadly killer, is then given off as a by-product. To maintain a safe environment in the shelter, be sure all furnaces and heating devices are vented properly. Open the door or window a crack to keep a fresh supply of oxygen flowing through the area. If you feel groggy or unusually sleepy, head outside immediately and breathe fresh air. Extra precautions are required in shanties where spearing is being done since the structure will probably be sealed tightly to prevent light from coming in.

Wooden shanties are large and heavy; a vehicle is usually used to transport it onto the ice. Be careful in early winter, when the ice might not be thick enough. Get the shelter off well before the ice starts deteriorating in the spring. More than one angler has lost a vehicle *and* a shanty by waiting too long to haul it off the ice. Fortunately, many states now have regulations which spell out a date when shelters must be off the ice. This is a logical way to ensure that the diehards and procrastinators get their structures on the shore, even if the fish are biting like heck!

Warmth and Comfort on the Ice

No outdoor activity is enjoyable if the participants are uncomfortable. The mind can't be satisfied unless the body is. Since icefishing is a winter sport, special care must be taken to provide basic body comforts. This is especially true since it is done from a stationary position. Unlike other outdoor sports, there's no opportunity to exercise while participating.

One day, as a teenager, I bicycled to a lake with five tip-ups and a bucket of minnows in the basket over the handlebars. It was unseasonably warm, and I wasn't dressed for extremely cold weather. Fishing was good; I wasn't in a hurry to leave when the sun sank below the horizon. As soon as the sun disappeared I began to shiver. The fish kept biting, so I stubbornly refused to go home. Ten minutes later I shivered so violently that I realized I'd be in trouble if I stayed much longer.

I pulled my tip-ups, loaded up my equipment, and decided to build a quick fire to warm my fingers that were almost numb. I had difficulty getting a pack of matches from my pocket, and when I finally did I couldn't move my hands enough to rip off a match. At that point I knew I'd better find some heat quickly, so I jumped on my bicycle and rode a half mile to a gas station. It seemed to take forever to thaw out, but I suffered no serious consequences except for two fingers that appeared to be frostbitten.

Several years later I helped a companion drag a buck out of woods in the Adirondack Mountains. The temperature was bitterly cold, and I learned later that it registered −32° F. I lost a glove in the snow while dragging the deer, and the same two fingers suffered frostbite again. They ached and felt numb for several days afterward.

Be prepared for any eventuality. When someone suffers from exposure, it's usually a person that isn't prepared, or someone who does something foolish. People who live in extremely cold areas suffer much less than those who live in a more temperate climate. Someone from a mild climate who ventures out on a frozen lake is more apt to get cold than a native from International Falls, Minnesota, for example. The Minnesota native doesn't have a higher body temperature, he just knows how to dress for cold weather and is aware of the fickle ways of winter. He won't venture out on a balmy day with minimal clothing because he knows how fast the weather can change. One who isn't used to such winter climate may be fooled by a few hours of sunshine. In the winter, cold fronts can move in rapidly, making life miserable for unprepared fishermen. As I learned the hard way, the disappearance of the sun quickly transforms a pleasant day into a bitter cold one.

Experienced outdoorsmen know that it's easy to take off excess clothes when they are warm, but it's tough to get warm if no more clothes are available. This should be heeded by every icefisherman. Little energy is expended, except for walking out on the ice and cutting holes. It's tough to keep warm while sitting still, so it's always wise to wear plenty of winter clothing.

The art of cutting a hole is a temporary part of ice angling, but it can have lasting effects that may ruin the entire day. As I just mentioned, this is one time when energy is expended while icefishing. A person can perspire if he works at it with more zeal and enthusiasm than necessary. When the body sweats, clothes that come in contact with the skin become moist. Later, as the person relaxes, the wet clothes begin to chill the outer portion of the body. Before long, shivering begins. Unless heat is available, fishing loses its enjoyment.

Some people sweat easily by performing relatively simple acts, even in winter weather. In this case, it might be worth while to purchase a power auger, or to find a youngster who owns one and pay him to cut your holes.

A shanty equipped with a heater is the answer to staying comfortable on the ice. However, for every angler who uses a shanty, many others do not. Proper clothing is essential to staying warm on a frozen lake.

An old saying commonly heard around Northern woodsmen goes like this, "If your feet are cold, put on your hat." This logic originates from the fact that a disproportionate amount of heat generated by the body can be lost when the head is exposed to cold weather.

Though the head has an adequate blood supply, it also has the most sensitive areas that are vulnerable to the cold. The nose and ears are readily frostbitten, and the eyes, cheeks, chin, and forehead are quite sensitive to cold temperatures.

A beard and moustache can have practical values in winter. They keep facial areas warm wherever hair growth is present. A person with a thick crop of hair on his head will be better protected than a balding individual. The saying "Bald is beautiful" might have application elsewhere in society, but it's a disadvantage on the ice!

A head covering is mandatory in cold weather. Thankfully, there are all kinds of possibilities in the headwear category. Different styles, colors, and materials offer a wide selection. The watch cap used by merchant seamen is popular among knowledgeable outdoorsmen. The cap, made of tightly knit 100 percent virgin wool, features the traditional cuff that pulls down and covers the forehead, ears, and neck. Face masks that cover the entire head are effective in cold, windy situations. Since they cover the mouth and nose, air is prewarmed and isn't a shock to the lungs. This also conserves the body heat that is normally lost when cold air is breathed. Face masks are especially good for active children who breathe deeply while running and playing about on the ice. Insulated hoods attached to parkas are excellent head coverings, although they're somewhat bulky. Many jackets with noninsulated hoods are acceptable windbreakers when worn over a watch cap or hat.

Danny Zumbo is suitably dressed for cold weather. The face mask helps to prevent frostbite, and the gloves and warm boots protect the extremities.

Ears need special protection. They offer a great deal of surface to the cold, and are thin and susceptible. Frostbitten ears are common in cold climates, but proper head apparel, available everywhere, should prevent this discomfort.

In extremely cold situations the nose not only suffers frostbite, but actually freezes inside the nostrils as well. I vividly remember an experience in New York's Adirondacks, one of the country's coldest areas. I was studying forestry at Paul Smith's College, and had just returned to campus from a weekend at home. Because of huge snowdrifts and deep snow, I had to park my car about a quarter mile from the dormitory. It was about 11 P.M. and exceedingly cold, but I didn't know how cold until I heard the radio report the next morning. By the time I walked from my car to the dormitory, my nose was actually glazed with ice just inside the nostril openings. I suffered no ill effects, but the feeling was uncomfortable. The temperature, as I later learned, was −44° F.

Ice anglers can always stay home on days that are bitterly cold, but many don't realize that windchill factors can adjust the effects of the cold and wind to extremely low levels.

Eyes suffer strain due to the bright glare of ice and snow. Sunglasses provide relief, and are especially useful to persons whose eyes are sensitive to bright light. Ski goggles offer even more protection if the wind is blowing, since tiny particles of ice and crusted snow can sting the face when carried by strong winds.

The neck is best protected by a scarf unless a parka hood is attached. Incidentally, a long scarf should never be allowed to dangle around when there's a chance it can be entangled around the moving parts of a power auger or snowmobile.

Feet require extra protection during cold weather. When feet are cold, the rest of the body is at least uncomfortable. Winter anglers must stand on ice, and this must be considered when selecting cold-weather footwear.

Feet become cold in three basic ways. Cold is transmitted through the soles from the ice, it enters through the sidewalls of the boot itself, and, when heat is lost through other parts of the body, it is pulled internally from the lower extremities into the upper torso.

In order to prevent cold feet, boot manufacturers have designed multitudes of boots. All types of insulations, fabrics, and designs have been incorporated into footwear in an attempt to solve the age-old problem of cold feet. Some types work, and others don't. Some people love a certain kind of boot while others hate it. No two individuals are alike: everyone has their own tolerance to cold, and everybody's feet are different.

No all-purpose boot meets all footwear requirements. Indeed, some boots are great for walking in snow, some are ideal for hiking across mountain ranges, and others are excellent when standing still. Boots are made of rubber, leather, vinyl and other materials. They can be short, tall, medium, insulated, and uninsulated. Most are waterproof, some have inner liners, and others offer unique breathing capabilities that assist in the elimination of perspiration.

With this assortment to select from, the ice angler must evaluate his particular needs. Will a snowmobile be used to get to the fishing site? Is a heated shanty available? How much exposure to bitter cold temperatures can be expected? Is the ice slushy and wet? All these questions should be asked to determine the best boot for the situation.

One of the biggest mistakes to make is to wear the same boot everywhere. I've seen Westerners wear thin-walled cowboy boots during extremely cold days, and walk off the ice prematurely because they can no longer endure the great discomfort and pain of cold, wet feet. I've seen Easterners try to enjoy an outing on the ice with uninsulated hiking boots that are practically worthless during cold weather, especially when they are in constant contact with ice. These boots might be plenty warm when hiking or climbing because the feet are being exercised, but they are likely to be dismal failures when circulation is slow.

My favorite boots have rubber bottoms with leather uppers. Felt liners are inserted into the boot cavity. They absorb perspiration and provide good insulation. These boots are a bit cumbersome for extensive walking, but they're ideal for keeping dry and warm on the ice. The felt liners (which are an integral feature of these boots) can be removed each evening to dry. Then they can be replaced when the boots are to be worn again. This type of boot isn't rare on the ice. I've noticed that the majority of anglers use them, regardless of the region.

Mukluks may be the warmest boots, but they aren't yet really popular in the continental United States. I have a pair made out of foam rubber, and I have yet to get cold feet while wearing them. Unfortunately, they're practically impossible to walk in. The best way to use them is to toss them in the snow sled and put them on after arriving at the fishing area.

Moisture is your feet's greatest enemy, whether it's produced

This is a favorite type of boot with icefishermen. Uppers are made from full-grain cowhide. Lowers are special rubber. Felt liners can be removed for drying. *Photo courtesy of L.L. Bean, Inc.*

through your pores as perspiration, or enters from outside the boot. Boots absolutely must be waterproof when used by ice anglers. Rubber boots need little care, but leather types must be constantly massaged with various waterproofing agents made specifically for that purpose. Even the best quality waterproof boots will leak if not treated correctly. Good boots are like guns—they need to be babied and cared for in order to work properly.

It's a mistake to put on cold boots and expect your feet to warm them, especially in extreme temperatures. Be sure boots are warm and dry before wearing them. Don't leave them outside. If you expect to wear them the next day, remove the liners immediately and place the boots in a warm spot. Never set them close to fireplaces, furnaces, or other sources of high heat. It's okay to place them in the vicinity of a heat source, but not too close.

When buying boots, be sure that they'll comfortably accommodate the socks you intend to wear. This usually means one size longer, and one size wider, than normal dress shoes. Wear heavy socks when trying on boots to ensure a correct fit. Boots that are too tight won't allow the freedom of movement required by the toes. Loose boots might allow the foot to slide and turn; this increases the possibility of blisters and sores. Boots that fit well should allow the toes to flex comfortably and should be snug enough so that the foot doesn't raise off the sole when the extremity is lifted.

Socks are important in keeping feet warm. Socks are frequently put on with no thought to comfort and warmth. They should be dry, clean, and the correct size. Socks that are too large may wrinkle inside the boot or bunch up. Too-small socks will prevent necessary toe movement. Some individuals prefer to wear a light cotton sock covered by warm wool socks, or two or three pairs of medium-weight socks. It makes little difference, as long as the foot fits well in the boot. Trial and error is the best way to determine the proper use of socks for individual comfort.

Sometimes it's impossible to prevent the build-up of foot moisture due to perspiration. When this happens, it's refreshing to change into warm, dry socks. It's always a good idea to bring along extra socks for a quick change on the ice.

Cold hands are always a handicap on the ice. Hands are easy to warm because they can be inserted into pockets, into gloves, or warmed over a heater or fire. Proper precautions should be taken however, to keep hands and fingers as comfortable as possible.

A wide variety of gloves and mittens is available to keep the hands warm. Gloves offer flexibility since each finger is allowed freedom of movement; mittens provide greater comfort because more body heat is generated by all parts of the hand. Most anglers use gloves when performing chores that require dexterity, and mittens when it's time to lounge around a bit waiting for a tip-up to fly its flag.

Hand apparel should fit properly. Liners can be used when the temperature is bitterly cold; fur or down gloves can be worn for the same purpose. Expensive dress gloves shouldn't be used when icefishing, they could be soiled with fish blood, slime, or residues from various baits.

A cheap pair of gloves can be used to take fish off the hook or to handle minnows. They'll get wet and dirty, but in icefishing *something* must. It might as well be inexpensive gloves.

Mittens should be somehow attached to the jacket so they won't accidentally fall into the snow. Mittens are efficient hand warmers, and they should be kept as dry as possible.

Hands should be kept out of icy water. A ladle or scoop is the best way to clear chunks of ice out of a freshly cut hole. A small aquarium net is ideal to retrieve a lively minnow out of a bait bucket. Fish should be handled only when necessary—an old rag or towel is useful to clean slime or moisture off of the hands.

Underwear is an important part of keeping warm. In the old days, flannel and cotton longjohns were common undergarments. Today fishermen wear thermal knit and insulated underwear. Even goose down is worn by discriminating folks who want the best.

I have several pairs of thermal and insulated longjohns, and start wearing them during duck season. By the time icefishing time arrives, I have a good idea of what I need to keep warm. The thermals are good for temperatures down to $-10°$ F., but I want insulated undergarments when it's zero or below. Sometimes I wear a combination of the two.

Outer garments vary widely—every style, material, and design can be seen on the ice. A heavy wool jacket is excellent protection from the cold, and is the best material to wear if the clothing is apt to get wet. Wool soaks up the moisture but still keeps the body warm, unlike any other material. Despite this advantage, wool doesn't stop enough wind when it's blowing on a cold day. I wear a light windbreaker over a sturdy woolen jacket. Many veteran outdoorsmen wouldn't think of wearing anything else besides wool, regardless of the activity. I've often seen the familiar red-and-black wool hunting jackets and trousers double as icefishing togs.

Comfort is an essential part of winter fishing, and these anglers are dressed for comfort. Note that they are fishing in a swath that has been plowed clear of deep snow. *Photo courtesy of Bob Gilsvik.*

Down remains a popular garment filler because of it's ability to trap and hold body heat. High-quality goose down is great, but its cost has been skyrocketing. Because of this expense factor, some companies substitute duck down for goose down. Some down that is sold is not down at all, but fluffy feathers that make a poor substitute.

Goose down is usually specified in the garment when it's used. Look for the actual volume of down in the article of clothing. This should be spelled out in pounds and ounces! When selecting a down jacket, look carefully at the stitching that baffles the fabric. If the stitching goes entirely through the garment from the outside to the inside, this is a sign of poor construction. There will be a weak spot at the point of stitching where no down is sewed in. If the stitching does not match on the outside and inside, then the down uniformly fills the entire garment with no voids.

Despite down's superior rating as a quality fabric, it's almost worthless when wet. Even the best outdoor filler has its shortcomings.

Many synthetic fillers on the market today are excellent substitutes for down, at a fraction of the price. Most of them are acceptable for ice angling, and many are rated as to the protection they offer at various temperatures.

Snowmobile suits are popular on the icefishing scene these days. The garments are designed for very cold temperatures, especially since the wind-chill factor is a constant concern. These suits are usually one piece, and zipper up through the middle. They're bulky and somewhat unwieldy, but they're great in harsh weather. It's tough to cut holes and perform other chores when wearing these suits, so it's advisable to take the garment off to avoid perspiring. Snowmobile suits are usually worn over regular shirts and trousers, so one shouldn't suffer from the cold if the suit is removed for a few minutes.

One-piece coveralls are fairly popular among winter anglers, but they don't offer the protection that snowmobile suits do. They aren't as bulky, and allow much more movement and flexibility. These garments work best when the temperature is around freezing.

The very best winter clothing in the world is the arctic garment designed for servicemen in the polar regions. This clothing will protect humans under the worst possible conditions, and would be welcomed by serious ice anglers. The drawback is its availability. These garments are practically impossible to purchase in the usual

Another group of anglers suitably dressed for the conditions of weather and ice. Panfish are the quarry at this Michigan lake. *Photo courtesy of Michigan Travel Commission.*

retail outlets. However, comparable suits are manufactured by companies that design clothing for mountaineering and expedition work. The cost, of course, is very high.

Jeans, dungarees, or denims are definitely off-limits on the ice. Denim absorbs water quickly and retains it. The fabric is loosely woven and allows wind to carry away warm air that otherwise should remain trapped between clothing and the body. It's almost worthless when it's wet, and even worse when it freezes.

There are all kinds of ways to stay comfortable on the ice. The hand warmer fits conveniently into a pocket; it's about as big as a pack of cigarettes. It's a quick source of heat, and is ideal for warming fingers after exposing them to icy water or air. Another handy item is a pair of battery-operated electric socks. These are invaluable for people who never seem to be able to keep their feet warm.

Feet get cold because of direct contact with ice. A little trick to avoid this contact is to bring along a discarded piece of carpet or even a burlap bag. By standing on this material, the transfer of cold from the ice to the boot is almost entirely eliminated. Try it—it works!

External sources of heat are always welcome on the ice, especially on a bone-chilling day when the sun is hidden behind clouds. All kinds of portable heaters are commercially available. Many anglers construct a special compartment in their ice sled for the heater, and leave it in the sled while it's operating.

Some winter fishermen build fires on the ice, but this should be avoided. One of the reasons is safety. If the ice is thin, the fire may melt it to the point where it will collapse if someone inadvertently steps too close. Fire debris is never attractive, and it becomes a center for trash as people toss cans, cartons, and bottles into the ashes.

Carry along a five-gallon pail, and build a fire in it. The heat will remain concentrated and the metal can will transmit heat evenly around it. A few big chunks of coal or a few pieces of hardwood will last for several hours. When it's time to go home, the pail can be cooled with ice water and taken off the lake with no more evidence than a shallow circle melted into the ice where it rested.

This chapter hasn't dealt with hypothermia, the deadly winter killer. Since this condition causes severe consequences, it will be discussed in detail in the chapter "Ice Safety."

Part of the secret of staying comfortable on the ice is to eat lots of calories. During a lull in the action, these anglers stoke up on hot venison stew.

WIND CHILL INDEX

WIND SPEED MPH	WHAT THE THERMOMETER READS (degrees F.)											
	50	40	30	20	10	0	—10	—20	—30	—40	—50	—60
	WHAT IT EQUALS IN ITS EFFECT ON EXPOSED FLESH											
CALM	50	40	30	20	10	0	—10	—20	— 30	— 40	— 50	— 60
5	48	37	27	16	6	— 5	—15	—26	— 36	— 47	— 57	— 68
10	40	28	16	4	— 9	—21	—33	—46	— 58	— 70	— 83	— 95
15	36	22	9	— 5	—18	—36	—45	—58	— 72	— 85	— 99	—112
20	32	18	4	—10	—25	—39	—53	—67	— 82	— 96	—110	—121
25	30	16	0	—15	—29	—44	—59	—74	— 88	—104	—118	—133
30	28	13	— 2	—18	—33	—48	—63	—79	— 94	—109	—125	—140
35	27	11	— 4	—20	—35	—49	—67	—82	— 98	—113	—129	—145
40	26	10	— 6	—21	—37	—53	—69	—85	—100	—116	—132	—148
Little danger if properly clothed					Danger of freezing exposed flesh			Great danger of freezing exposed flesh				

Source: U. S. Army

This chart tells you the effects of various combinations of wind speed and air temperature. It's obvious why proper clothing and some sort of shelter are essential to your comfort on the ice.

Ice Safety

An ice-covered lake offers a unique opportunity to human beings. It offers a means of traveling on top of a body of water. All too often, though, people place too much trust in the supportive layer of ice. Tragic accidents occur every year. In almost every case, people were overconfident of the ability of the ice to sustain their weight, or that of their vehicles.

There are widely publicized standards that indicate the weight that various ice thicknesses can support. Here is the table:

Ice thickness	**Maximum weight prescribed**
2 inches	One person on foot
3 inches	Group, in single file
7 1/2 inches	Automobile (2 tons gross)
8 inches	Light truck (2 1/2 tons gross)
10 inches	Medium truck (3 1/2 tons gross)
12 inches	Heavy truck (8 tons gross)
15 inches	10 tons
20 inches	25 tons

These weights are applicable to clear, blue ice. Slush and snow ice is half as strong as clear ice, so the thicknesses in the above table should be doubled if poor-quality ice is present. Black, honeycombed ice is typical in the spring just prior to ice out. One should never travel on this ice, regardless of the necessity.

Another ice safety rule that I learned in Boy Scouts goes like this: one inch, keep off; two inches, one may; three inches, small groups; four inches, okay.

A good share of ice breakthroughs occur in early and late season. Anxious anglers who can't wait venture out on newly formed ice, assuming it's strong enough. This is a foolish attitude, and the participants might pay dearly.

Fishing through crystal-clear ice always gives me a weird feeling because I'm constantly reminded that there's a lot of water beneath me. When ice is snow covered, I think we tend to treat it with more apathy than usual. The old saying "ignorance is bliss" has no value to those who travel on ice. This attitude gets people into serious trouble.

Early, thin ice is doubly dangerous because veteran anglers know that most fish are at their best behavior during the first few weeks that ice forms. Consequently, eager fishermen head for the lakes earlier to take advantage of this peculiar behavior pattern. The reasons why fish bite well under first ice are only speculative. Some anglers feel that since there's usually a break between fall fishing and the formation of new ice, the fish are rested and see no lures or baits for a several week period. The first ice anglers who make offerings tempt the fish when they're unwary and vulnerable.

Another opinion has it that since ice lures are designed differently than standard open water lures, fish are actually attracted to them because of their unusual shapes and behavior.

Since ice anglers who fish lakes early in the season generally reap attractive quantities of fish, safety must be an important consideration.

The period just before ice-out sometimes proves to be highly productive. Some anglers theorize that fish go on a feeding campaign very late in the winter to replace fats that are lost through the cold period, when little or no growth takes place. Anglers who note an increase in fishing success during this period keep coming back to the lake, despite the fact that ice deterioration is well under way. No fish is worth the possibility of plunging through rotten ice.

Fickle winter weather may render ice unsafe through the entire season in areas that normally receive cold temperatures. The famous drought that affected the West during the winter of 1976-77 kept many lakes open because of the unseasonably warm weather.

A curious situation developed on Utah's Willard Bay during that drought period. Some anglers learned that the crappies in the lake would bite through the ice. Willard Bay is a new lake, and crappies were just getting a good start. Most were being taken during the spring months. Word of the new winter fishery got around, and thousands of anglers suddenly appeared on the ice to seek the panfish. There were several open leads throughout the lake and thin spots were common because of the drought. Before the winter was over, 25,000 angler days had been spent on the ice, but not without tragedy. Thirty-nine people fell through the ice; one person died.

A friend of mine witnessed a man who fell through. The luckless individual approached an area of black, honeycombed ice and proceeded to walk directly over it. Several onlookers yelled and warned him to detour but he paid no attention and kept right on going.

Suddenly he plunged through the ice into deep water. He bobbed up, grabbed onto the edge of the ice, and broke through again. Three times he tried to crawl up on the ice, but he failed each time. Finally he reached strong ice and was able to hang on until rescuers passed him a rope. It was learned later that the man had never been on a frozen lake before, and knew nothing about ice.

There are times when good judgment is required to determine the safety of ice. Since the ice-safety table refers only to clear, blue ice, it has no application at all to other types of ice. That's when common sense is important.

River ice, for example, is 15 percent weaker than lake ice. According to the Coast Guard, saltwater ice is safe only when it has a pure white or bluish cast. Even lake ice is seldom uniform in thickness because of many factors, including eroding currents, melting action of springs, and the inflow of warm water.

Before venturing onto a frozen lake, always examine the ice carefully. Measure the thickness at several points. Be wary of open leads, cracked areas, spring holes, and thin spots. Take extra precautions if snow covers the ice; it's impossible to recognize telltale weak areas when they're covered by a blanket of snow.

When a frozen lake takes in more water than goes out, it must obviously store this extra water under the ice. The shoreline ice will begin breaking up, and the excess water seeps up along the entire perimeter. The water runs along the ice close to shore and either refreezes or forms slush, especially when there's a covering of snow. Open leads may be common close to the shore. This situation may present a sticky problem, since the ice throughout 95 percent of the lake may be 2 feet thick and safe enough to hold an 18-wheeler, but totally inaccessible for the first few yards.

A solution is to find a spot where the span can be crossed, or by walking on a dock or pier which leads directly to safe ice. Lay some boards across the weak spot so the weight is equally distributed.

Many lakes in the West are filled to capacity while they're frozen over, because there are no irrigation needs in the winter. Upstream water sources flow directly into the lakes rather than being diverted to agricultural areas. As a result, many lowland lakes in the West have weak shorelines during winter. When inflow exceeds outflow, the extra water simply pushes up around the shoreline. When inflow is less than outflow, the ice forms a mantle and may no longer be in contact with the water.

Lakes that lose more water than they take in may actually cause the ice to bridge the surface of the lake so there's an air space between ice and water. This is especially true in ponds and smaller lakes, but it's been known to happen in big waters. When this occurs, even the thickest ice may be unsafe. Unless ice is directly supported by water underneath, it is treacherous. There are no exceptions.

Many frozen lakes have large expanses of open water. Constant wind action sometimes restricts ice formation, and only the calmer areas freeze over. When this occurs, stay away from the open water. Constant erosion by lapping waves eats away the top of the ice edge as well as the bottom.

Despite all precautions, there might come a time when disaster strikes and you fall through the ice. What do you do?

If there are people within shouting distance, get their attention. Scream as loudly as you can and wave an arm while holding onto the edge of the ice with the other hand.

Remain as calm as you can, but this is easier said than done. Don't lunge frantically at the edge of the broken hole, because your weight will probably break off another chunk and you'll go down again. There's also the possibility that your body might jackknife under the rim of the ice.

Experts suggest that you extend your arms forward over the unbroken surface and kick your legs as vigorously as you can. This will lift the lower part of your torso and will help propel you onto solid ice. If more ice breaks off, try again. When you finally get your chest onto safe ice, squirm, wiggle, or roll away from the hole.

If you're prepared, you'll have a pair of ice awls to help you get out. Jab each awl as far up onto the unbroken ice as you can, kick your legs, and try to pull yourself out. If you don't have awls, grab anything you have that's made out of metal, and use it to help you get a firm hold on the solid ice. Reach into your pockets and extract whatever you can find: car keys, a pocket knife, fingernail clipper, a pen. Your belt buckle will work if you can't find anything else. Another possibility is your glasses. Fold the ear pieces in, grasp the glasses in the middle, and stab the ice with the pointed end. Don't worry about breaking the glass and cutting your hand. There's more at stake than cuts and bruises.

One man who couldn't find any other way out of a break reached out and let his mittens freeze to solid ice. When they froze tightly enough, he simply pulled himself up far enough and rolled free. This individual displayed rare calm—a trait that only a few people possess.

Remember that extremely cold water quickly absorbs body heat and is apt to cause shock. Studies show that in freezing water, a human may have less than 15 minutes to live. It's imperative to make the first few efforts count. Rather than making several half-hearted attempts, take a rest and give it a super effort. If that fails, rest for a few more moments and try again.

Suppose that someone else falls through and *you're* the rescuer. What should you do? Do *not* dash over and extend a helping hand to the victim. An attempt of that sort exposes the rescuer to needless danger and makes him less effective. Chances are good that he could end up in the hole with the person he's trying to rescue. According to the Red Cross, here's the procedure to follow:

"First, and most important, don't panic.

Regardless of how many onlookers are present, somebody should immediately go to the nearest phone and summon help from the police and fire departments.

Only a few rescuers who know what they are doing should actually participate. Extra people milling about not only add confusion but often put such a strain on the ice that they end up in the water, too.

Keep a safe distance from the victim since you can break through, too. If the victim is near shore, you can use what experts call an 'extension rescue'. Lie down to distribute your weight over a large area, inch toward the victim, and extend to him a long stick, pole, plank, or ladder.

Toss him a rope. Tying a branch or other object to the victim's rope end makes it easier for you to throw, and gives him something to hold onto. Or, tie a loop on the end of the rope you intend to throw to him. If his hands are too numb to hold on to the rope, instruct him to slip the loop over his head and under his armpits so he can be physically hauled out. If no actual rope is available, make one by tying together coats, towels, scarves, belts—anything that's handy.

If the victim can't be reached in the ways described above, form a human chain. Each member should lie flat on the ice, holding onto the ankles of the person in front. They should worm their way toward the victim, with the leader grasping the victims wrists; then the whole line wriggles backward over the ice, drawing the victim to safety. If the weak ice gives way, dunking the leader, the others can pull him out.

Never stand up near the ice break. If you approach, your weight *must* be distributed over as much ice as possible. This means the prone position—nothing less.

A spare tire from a car trunk can be rolled to the scene. It will float and support the weight of five persons in the water."

It's bad enough to break through a spot of weak ice, but totally unnecessary to fall into a hole made by an icefisherman. This happens frequently, however. Fortunately, people who step into holes can usually catch themselves before going all the way through. The ice will probably be safe around the hole, and won't hamper efforts to get out. Many states have found solutions to this problem by placing a limit on the maximum size of the hole. Ten to twelve inches is the usual size limit.

I've seen people cut holes that would accommodate a 55-gallon drum. They were fishing for yellow perch. Big holes are usually the case when axes are used to chop ice. These tools work poorly, but many folks don't own ice augers or chisels and have no other tool. This is especially true in the West where icefishing is new in many areas.

A few years ago I watched a group of university students as they scuba-dived under a frozen lake. They used an entry hole that measured 4 feet by 6 feet. I wondered how they were going to close off the hole. They later carried pieces of plywood out and covered the hole. With the plywood in place, they erected a sign that said "danger" and hung orange streamers from it. Several days later, when the ice had thickened in the hole, they removed the plywood.

It's common courtesy to warn people of extra large holes and weak spots. You'd want someone to tell you of unknown dangers, so it's always a good idea to get the word out to anyone who comes near.

Some people take chances on marginal ice if they're wearing skis. It's true that skis distribute weight over a wider area, but if the ice is questionable enough to require the use of skis, stay off it completely.

Driving on ice with snowmobiles and cars requires strong, thick ice. Snowmobiles are discussed in more detail later in this book because they're exceedingly popular among ice anglers these days. Driving an auto on the ice of *any* lake is never recommended by safety organizations, but it's done every day on extremely thick ice. I've seen school buses on ice that were converted to camping units, as well as 70-foot mobile homes! Camp trailers and motor homes are also common.

Driving a car on the ice takes some courage for somebody who has never done it before. It's an eerie feeling, especially when the ice rumbles and groans underneath. I made my debut in driving on ice at Lake Champlain. I was scared to death, and the only reason I continued was because several dozen cars were already there. I still drove with the door open, and prepared to bail out in case the automobile broke through.

On some lakes, cars are a fact of life, and few people consider going icefishing unless they can drive to the door of their shanty. On Mille Lacs Lake, Minnesota, it's been estimated that 3,000 to 5,000 cars are on the ice during popular weekends. There are dozens of other lakes throughout Minnesota, Wisconsin, and Michigan where thousands of automobiles are on the ice at one time.

It is estimated that upwards of 500 vehicles break through the ice every year. Most of these accidents occur when drivers take foolish chances. Many cars crash through early and late in the ice season when ice isn't as strong as it should be. Other breakthroughs occur when the vehicle hits a thin spot.

In popular ice fishing areas, many anglers use "ice buggies" that are old, stripped-down vehicles customized especially for ice travel. Most have the doors removed for quick evacuation in case of a breakthrough.

When driving on ice, remember to get out of the vehicle immediately. This obviously rules out the use of safety belts. Don't even *think* about using them. Instead, drive with the doors open for a quick exit. if your vehicle plunges through, take a flying leap off to the side. Most vehicles don't sink like a stone. Instead, the front end usually crashes through because it's heaviest. The rest of the vehicle slowly starts to settle. Some safety advisors recommend that before leaving the vehicle, put the car in neutral so the spinning tires don't drive it down quicker. This advice is sound, but few people will have the presence of mind to think about gear selection when their car is sinking!

If you can't jump out on the initial crunch, do so as the car is going down. In most cases, great chunks of ice will be floating around the car. These ice pieces will hinder your progress to reach firm ice, and you'll have to maneuver through them with care. The last thing you want to do is go under and have a big hunk of heavy ice prevent you from surfacing.

Tests made on sinking automobiles have determined that the average auto takes four to five minutes before sinking out of sight. In the majority of cases this allows plenty of time to get out the doors or windows.

Most fatalities involving car breakthroughs occur after the occupant gets safely out of the car, and not as a trapped victim after the car submerges. Once free of the car, the hapless individual is unable to get back on the ice, and ultimately drowns in the freezing water.

Many breakthroughs occur over shallow water less than 10 feet deep. If this is the case, stand on top of the submerged vehicle until help arrives. If no one is in sight, dog paddle to the edge of firm ice and try to climb out. If you fail, make your way back over the car and stand on it again while you rest for another attempt.

There are a few important rules to remember when driving on the ice. There are usually no lanes of travel, so you're free to aim the vehicle in any direction. When another car approaches you from the front, use the same rule that you would if you were on a highway, that is, stay to the right. If a car happens to be traveling aimlessly along with no obvious course in mind, slow down and let it move by. Don't follow a car too closely, and keep a safe distance from *any* car, regardless of whether it's parked or moving. A concentration of weight on the ice could create enough stress to cause a serious break. Always keep your speed down on ice.

It's always difficult to stop and maneuver on a frozen lake, especially at speeds that are too fast for the slippery surface. Be especially wary around shanties and groups of people. When approaching an ice angler, show him some courtesy by making a wide berth around him. He might get a bit nervous as your car rolls by, too close, or he might feel that moving automobiles spook fish under the ice. There are some folks who do.

When snowmobiles are traveling on ice, they need to be observed closely for a number of reasons. First, a child might be operating one and may not have good driving sense around automobiles. Second, snowmobiles sit low, and may be difficult to see from a car. Third, snowmobiles may change their course rapidly, and could be unpredictable.

Remember that the stopping distance on dry, cold ice is much shorter than on a wet, melting surface. If you're driving on a mild balmy day over watery ice, you'll have a harder time stopping than if it were zero degrees.

Snow or studded tires are acceptable for ice driving. Chains are a nuisance, and cause a bumpy ride. They're not worth putting on, unless there are slippery obstacles to negotiate in order to get onto the lake.

There are no special skills involved in driving on ice. Use good judgment, and you'll have no problem.

Hypothermia: Not long ago few people knew what hypothermia meant. It's now a household word that's used to describe the age-old tragedy of suffering from exposure.

Technically, hypothermia is the lowering of the temperature within the core of the body. Even a small loss of body temperature in the inner core can lead to death if not quickly treated. Hypothermia begins when cold external temperatures cause the body to constrict the surface blood vessels. This defensive maneuver permits more blood to flow to the brain as well as other internal organs. At the same time, the body tries to generate more heat by increasing its metabolic rate. As a result, the body begins to shiver, which is caused by the involuntary action of muscles to produce heat. Shivering is the first clue to hypothermia; death may occur less than two hours later.

Persons unfamiliar with hypothermia believe that sub-zero temperatures are required to cause it. This is untrue. Hypothermia can strike at temperatures as high as 45 to 50° F. Of course, lower temperatures will increase the chance of suffering from the dread condition. Wet clothing and wind are important factors whenever hypothermia strikes.

Icefishermen are good targets for hypothermia. Fortunately, most winter anglers dress warmly enough to protect themselves, but every year there are people who suffer needlessly from exposure. Some of the cases are fatal.

When your clothing becomes wet, even from excessive perspiration, be wary of rapid chilling. This is especially true if the wind is blowing, since the windchill factor causes the actual external temperature to plummet to extremes.

If you fall through the ice, take immediate steps to find warmth quickly when you get out. If necessary, knock on a shanty or cabin door to get close to heat. Don't worry about imposing on someone's privacy. It may mean your life.

Hypothermia can occur any time the body starts to get cold. If mild shivering suddenly becomes noticeable, don't laugh it off, get into some type of shelter, drink warm liquids, and change into dry clothes, if possible.

If you find yourself in a position where a person is showing advanced stages of hypothermia, act quickly. First, keep the person awake and force him to drink hot liquids. Strip the victim's clothes off entirely, and get him into a sleeping bag with another person who is also stripped. Body contact is a vital means of transferring critical heat to the victim. Don't worry about social or personal inhibitions at this point. This technique may be the only way to save a life.

The following symptoms occur as the body temperature begins to drop:

99 to 96° F.—Shivering becomes intense and uncontrollable. The ability to perform simple tasks is impaired.

95 to 91° F.—Shivering becomes violent. Difficulty in speaking. Skin color becomes pale.

90 to 86° F.—Shivering decreases and is replaced by rigidity in the muscles. Thinking is less clear, although victim seems to be able to maintain posture.

85 to 81° F.—Victim becomes irrational and may drift into stupor. Pulse weakens.

80 to 78° F.—Victim becomes unconscious. Heartbeat becomes erratic. Most reflexes cease to function.

Below 78° F.—Cardiac and respiratory failure. Little chance to revive victim. Death probable.

Frostbite is a common winter problem. Although not usually fatal, it can cause permanent damage. It normally occurs when extremities are exposed to cold wind and bitter temperatures. The best treatment for frostbite is to warm the affected area rapidly with warm water, around 100° F. Just a short time ago, it was believed that frostbite should be treated by rubbing the injury with snow or ice. Don't do it! This will only worsen the condition.

This chapter will not detail the techniques of reviving a victim who has apparently stopped breathing. This information is available from many sources, and it's wonderful to note that millions of Americans are capable of administering various resuscitation procedures.

One new development saves additional lives, however. It was brought to light by Dr. Martin J. Nemiroff, a Michigan physician, who studied 60 near-drowning incidents. One of these involved a 2-year-old boy who was found face down in a lake after having been missing for 20 minutes. The youngster recovered fully after prolonged mouth-to-mouth resuscitation by his mother. Most humans who are submerged for longer than 4 minutes are assumed to have suffered brain damage. The 2-year-old boy, however, showed no such effects afterward. Nemiroff's studies caused him to conclude that the boy would have probably died if he had fallen into a heated swimming pool instead of an icy lake. The child, he stated, was saved by the "diving reflex," an involuntary neural response that delays suffocation by diverting oxygen from the arteries to the heart, brain, and lungs. The reflex is triggered when the victim's face is submerged in cold water, and is strongest in infants and small children. Nemiroff suggests that it is first activated during labor when the oxygen supply to the fetus is reduced.

Out of 15 patients investigated by Nemiroff who were submerged in water for lengthy periods of time, 11 were revived without injury, two died of lung infections, and two sustained permanent brain damage because resuscitation efforts were mishandled or delayed. In one case, a patient was revived after 38 minutes under water.

Nemiroff urges rescuers to work vigorously on anyone who is submerged in cold water for less than an hour. He also feels that the cooler the water, and the younger the victim, the better his chances are to be revived.

A final word on ice safety involves the ability to carry and read a compass. This might sound ridiculous, but plenty of people become hopelessly lost on a frozen lake when the fog rolls in or a ground blizzard strikes. There are usually no reference points on ice, so a low-visibility situation lends itself to a hopeless predicament unless tracks in the snow can be followed back to the shoreline.

Before a storm front or fog bank moves in, take out the compass and point it north. Look to the shoreline where your vehicle is parked and check the compass to see what bearing to follow. If you walk off the ice when visibility is low, keep checking the compass and stay on the bearing you noted before. Eventually you'll arrive at your destination.

Snowmobiles

Winter recreation experienced a wholesale revolution when snowmobiles appeared in the 1960's. Snowmobiling is one of the fastest-growing winter activities in the United States and Canada. According to the International Snowmobile Industry Association, the number of snowmobiles sold each year jumped from 500 in 1960 to 235,000 in 1976. As of 1977, it has been estimated that over 5 million snowmobiles are owned by Americans and Canadians.

Snowmobiles also added a new dimension to ice fishing. Anglers quickly learned that big lakes could be traversed quickly via the new machines, and many fishing grounds were discovered that weren't known before. And, of course, those little jewels in the backcountry were no longer off-limits to ice fishermen. The snowmobile would take the angler practically anywhere.

In order to fully assess the impact of snowmobiles and their relationship to winter fishing, let's take a very basic look at the machines. The operation of a snowmobile may seem like a simple matter, but this attitude often gets the winter participant in trouble.

A snowmobile is a motorized vehicle that has a low-horsepower engine. It is designed for travel over ice and snow, *not* dry pavement, rocks, logs, grass and other non-snow materials. It is generally advised that at least four inches of snow be present to operate a snowmobile.

It is powered by a rubber or steel-cleated track, and is steered with handlebars that turn one or two skis in front of the vehicle. The machine is capable of carrying one to three people, depending on its size. Snowmobiles weigh 250 pounds or more, and have a fuel capacity of two to seven gallons.

It's imperative that the beginning snowmobile operator know the

Terry Larsen, a Utah Park Ranger, uses his snowmobile to check fishermen and also to aid in search and rescue. Here he's showing a pair of anglers a favorite bait.

basics of his machine. Children who use the vehicles where adults are not present should be taught how to cope with mechanical problems that are likely to occur. Every snowmobiler should become thoroughly familiar with the owner's manual before starting the machine for the first time.

Maintenance of the vehicle is necessary to keep it in running condition. There are few things more frustrating than a machine that is tough to start or one that stalls with disturbing frequency. Since a snowmobile is often driven at night, the headlights and tail lights should be checked prior to a ride that might continue into the dark hours. Most snowmobiles operate with a two-cycle engine, so it's important that the oil and gasoline mixture be correct for the engine specifications. Always follow the manufacturer's recommendations precisely when preparing fuel. The machines should never be refueled while the engine is running. Use a dip stick to check the level of the fuel—never an open flame. Keep open flames such as matches and cigarette lighters away from batteries where explosive gases can be emitted.

Minimum safety equipment includes properly functioning brake and steering systems, front and rear lights that are in working order and a rear-view mirror that is positioned correctly. Before setting out for a trip, check the brakes at slow speeds to make sure they are functioning properly. Likewise, test the steering components since chunks of ice or snow may prevent proper operation.

Emergency equipment includes a number of items that should be carried to meet unforeseen situations. A tool kit and first aid kit are necessary when snowmobiles are operated in backcountry areas. The reasons are obvious. A pair of snow shoes or skis are required for each passenger. These items become essential when a breakdown occurs in deep snow and no assistance is available. A rope is a useful item for towing a broken-down snowmobile, and a lightweight block-and-tackle is handy when trying to move a disabled vehicle. Other emergency items include an extra drive belt, a new set of spark plugs that are gapped properly, a supply of matches in a waterproof container, a flashlight, flares, extra fuel, a compass, and maps if a strange area is being traveled.

A novice snowmobiler shouldn't attempt difficult maneuvers with his vehicle until he has thoroughly familiarized himself with its operation, and has acquired a substantial background of basic snowmobiling. Each machine acts differently, so extra precautions should be taken to learn each vehicle's peculiarities. As a rule, snowmobiles have a hand-activated brake on the left handle bar. The brake is designed to slow down the machine gradually rather than to stop it instantly. Therefore, the brakes should be tested when the vehicle is operated on different surfaces, such as ice, wet snow, and dry snow.

It's important that snowmobile operators know the rules governing the use of their vehicles. Most states have specific regulations regarding the machines. If in doubt, snowmobile owners should contact the highway patrol or local police department. Further restrictions might be set by counties or municipalities. Learn the laws.

Snowmobile owners should also be aware of personal liability and property damage limitations that apply to themselves, their passengers, and their vehicle. Adequate insurance should cover these items.

When transporting a snowmobile, it's best to use a specially designed trailer that's made to accommodate the vehicle. Snowmobiles must be securely fastened whenever being trailered. Metal tie-downs that are bolted or welded to the trailer are the most satisfactory. For adequate protection, cover the snowmobile while in transit. This will prevent dust, road salt, mud, and dirt from fouling the moving parts.

Clothing for snowmobilers must be warm, reflective, and windproof, yet light and flexible enough so movement isn't impeded. Most snowmobile suits are well-made. Footwear and gloves should be insulated. These extremities will be exposed to moving air, so they must be well protected. Ski goggles or sunglasses should be worn on bright, sunny days. Snow and ice reflects a great deal of light, and the resulting glare can cause excessive eye discomfort and irritation.

A helmet or hard hat is advisable for the driver and passengers in the event of an accident.

In many areas, icefishermen join in groups and journey into the hinterlands for a day's angling on a remote lake. This is great fun, and is productive in terms of fishing, as well as offering plenty of camaraderie to those involved. To play it safe when traveling together, follow a few basic rules.

When moving single file, leave plenty of stopping room between vehicles. Remember, snowmobiles can't stop instantly. When traveling in wooded areas, slow down and watch for hazards such as snow-covered stumps, boulders, fallen trees, and branches. If driving across pastures, be alert for fences that may have a strand of barbed wire stretched across your path. This is especially important at night. Never attempt a safari into a remote area unless you're accompanied by a person who knows the area well. If Lost Lake is brimming with chunky rainbows—be sure you can find Lost Lake before traveling to it. When going uphill in a snowmobile, use a slight throttle reduction. If the path is steep, a "zig-zag" technique can be used to reach the top of the slope.

When going down a steep slope, keep the vehicle in gear and maintain a slight throttle pressure. Use the most direct route whenever possible and follow the fall-line of the terrain. Never travel at right angles to the slope. Always travel to remote areas on a buddy-buddy system. Don't attempt a shortcut alone, and frequently count all the members of the party to be sure someone isn't stalled far behind. Don't use alcoholic beverages before or during a snowmobile journey. The machines are as deadly as cars and motorcycles and should be handled as such. If you'd like a drink, do so after the snowmobile is parked in the back yard or adequately stored.

Since icefishermen use snowmobiles on ice, extra precautions are necessary. Be sure the ice will safely support your vehicle. If you memorized the ice safety table in Chapter 12, you know that three inches of ice will support a group walking single file. This *doesn't* apply to a snowmobile, even though the combined weight of a group of people can be much more than a snowmobile. During the beginning of the season, wait until the ice is uniformly six inches thick before venturing out on it with a machine. Note the word "uniformly." No lake has the same ice thickness along the entire surface. Thin spots are common, and slush ice might be covered by a layer of snow. Consider these possibilities when speeding across the open ice.

Be extra wary after dark. The headlight on your snowmobile won't give you much indication as to the condition of the ice in front of you. Don't overdrive your headlights. Be sure you can stop within the visual span afforded by the lights.

In northern Minnesota, a 32-year-old father took his son and three daughters on a skating and fishing outing with their snowmobile. While returning after dark on a lake that had 12 inches of ice on it, the vehicle plunged into open water and sank. All were drowned.

Most snowmobile enthusiasts are aware of the hazards of driving on ice. In fact, the safety pledge of an organization of several hundred snowmobile clubs says in part, "I will not cross or travel on frozen lakes and streams unless the ice is thick enough to support the weight of my snowmobile and my passengers. When traveling in new areas, I will seek advice on ice conditions. I will stay on marked trails or marked roads open to snowmobiles."

The U.S. Consumer Safety Commission estimates that approximately 18,000 persons were treated in hospital emergency rooms for injuries; most were lacerations and contusions. Sprains, strains, and fractures were also reported. About one-third of the emergency room victims had injuries which involved the lower extremities of the body; one-sixth involved the upper extremities. Almost one-fourth of the injuries involved the head and neck areas. Three out of four snowmobile victims were male, and the largest number of injuries were to victims aged 25 to 34.

In an earlier study, during the 1974-75 season, it was learned that 170 people were killed in snowmobile accidents. Of these, 23 fatalities occurred when machines broke through ice or were inadvertently driven into open water. Other causes of accidents included collisions with fixed objects; collisions with other snowmobiles, automobiles, and trains; and accidents involving unstable terrain in which victims drove off cliffs, were crushed by overturned vehicles, or were thrown from their machines.

So far this chapter has discussed snowmobile usage and safety. Now let's get into the practical aspects of snowmobiles and icefishing.

Your snowmobile can take you to areas you never dreamed of going. Distant areas on large lakes are accessible to snow machines, and are no longer too far to walk to. Fishing time is extended whenever snowmobiles are used because travel time to the fishing area is reduced. I remember one occasion when I fished New York's Oneida Lake for walleyes. The fishing grounds were about 1 1/2 miles from shore, and it took us over an hour to walk out to the best

Snowmobiles (the one in foreground has a matching trailer) can quickly haul passengers and gear to the fishing grounds. *Photo courtesy of Arctic Enterprises, Inc.*

area. Dozens of snowmobilers scooted past us and had fish flopping on the ice by the time we arrived at the grounds. That incident was enough to make me finally see the light. When I got home I purchased my first snowmobile!

In the West, as well as many other areas, many high-country lakes are open year-round to icefishing, but are out of reach to anyone who doesn't own a snowmobile, snowshoes, or cross-country skis. The latter two items are superb means of winter transportation, but involve a lengthier period of travel time.

Icefishing enthusiasts who use snowmobiles must get their necessary gear on the ice. This problem is easily solved by several possibilities. One is a rear-mounted cargo carrier that is bolted or strapped to the back of the machine. The carrier will accommodate a good deal of gear, but ice augers and minnow buckets might prove unweildy or cumbersome. The best bet is a tow or trail sled that is roomy enough to accept all required equipment. Some of these sleds fold up for easier storage, and some allow an extra passenger to sit

This snowmobile tows a homemade trailer that hauls plenty of gear to where the fish are. The fishermen exchange information about fishing strategies. *Photo courtesy of Michigan Travel Commission.*

or stand. If a homemade sled is being used, be sure it's sturdy, since it will sooner or later be riding on rough surfaces at various speeds. If you make your own trail sled, use wood screws rather than nails to gain more strength.

Snowmobiles are a welcome contribution to winter fishing. Treat them with respect, use good judgment and common sense, and don't make a pest out of yourself around other fishermen. You'll get much out of your machine and your sport if you use your head.

Snowshoes and Cross-Country Skis

Thousands of lakes and ponds in North America are unfished during winter because they're inaccessible. Snowmobiles changed this picture appreciably, as more winter anglers visit back-country lakes each year on these machines.

For some folks, though, the only way to travel on snow is via showshoes or cross-country skis. By doing so, they have a more intense appreciation for the natural world in its winter setting. There is more of a human element in this mode of transportation, too, since no gasoline-powered engine is available to provide the energy. It all comes from the legs, lungs, and muscles.

Snowshoes had their beginnings when early man learned he couldn't walk over deep snow without some kind of assistance. Pliable branches that could be bent into the proper shape provided the frames, and sinew was generally used for the mesh and lashings. The material used varied according to availability and local snow conditions.

Most snowshoes today are made of ash, with varnished cowhide stretched between the frames. Aluminum and plastic snowshoes are appearing on the market, but the wooden models remain the most popular among experts.

Snowshoes operate on the principle of spreading weight out over a broad surface. Under certain conditions, it takes a great deal of effort to travel with snowshoes, especially when the snow is powdery and deep. When this is the case, the snowshoes are apt to plunge through the top 12 inches of snow before reaching a solid base. Snow-shoeing becomes tedious in this situation, because loose snow is usually lifted up on top of the shoe at each step, and the legs must be moved almost straight up and down. This is tiresome on unused muscles, but it's part of the sport.

Snowshoeing is easy to learn. No schools, lessons, or special skills are required to learn how to walk on snowshoes. A back yard or city park is the best place to practice walking. The average person needs little more than a half hour of practice to get the hang of it.

A long, gliding walk usually works best. The snowshoes shouldn't be lifted high above the surface of the snow with each step, but should be slid forward. As the heel rises with the forward stride, the toe turns down through the toe pocket of the framework. Be aware that snowshoeing makes some heavy demands on your calf muscles. A beginner will feel some muscle soreness and tightness after the first trials. This is only a minor hindrance if compared to the aches and pains generated when snowshoes *aren't* worn in deep snow situations.

I first wore snowshoes when studying forestry in the Adirondacks. During the late winter, my classmates and I managed a maple-syrup operation and were required to gather the buckets of sap that hung on the trees. It would have been an impossible task to travel through the woods without snowshoes, since the snow was at least four feet deep.

Later on, I used the snowshoes to walk to a lake that had a reputation for producing big northern pike. It was the first time I'd used them for icefishing, and my efforts were rewarded with three fish that weighed 12 pounds each.

There are several different types of snowshoes, and all are designed with terrain, vegetation, and the type of walking as the primary considerations.

The Maine Snowshoe is one of the most popular, and is a good compromise snowshoe. It's adapted for most any kind of travel, including long trips and moderately brushy situations. The snowshoe comes in various sizes, depending on the wearer's weight. Recommended sizes are as follows: Persons weighing 100 to 125 pounds—12 inches × 42 inches; 125 to 165 pounds—13 inches × 48 inches; 165 to 225 pounds—14 inches × 48 inches. Childrens sizes are: 45 to 70 pounds—10 inches × 36 inches; 75 to 95 pounds—11 inches × 40 inches.

The Pickerel Snowshoe is a long, narrow shoe that is adapted for lengthy trips of several miles. The length and design of the shoe allows for easy striding. A disadvantage is the difficulty of maneuvering in thick vegetation. In brushy situations, the shoe may be cum-

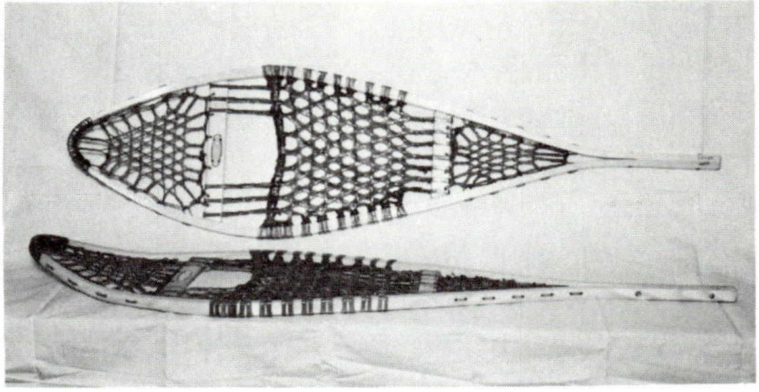

The Maine snowshoe is one of the most popular styles. It's used for long-distance walking as well as for traveling in moderately dense brush. *Photo courtesy of L.L. Bean, Inc.*

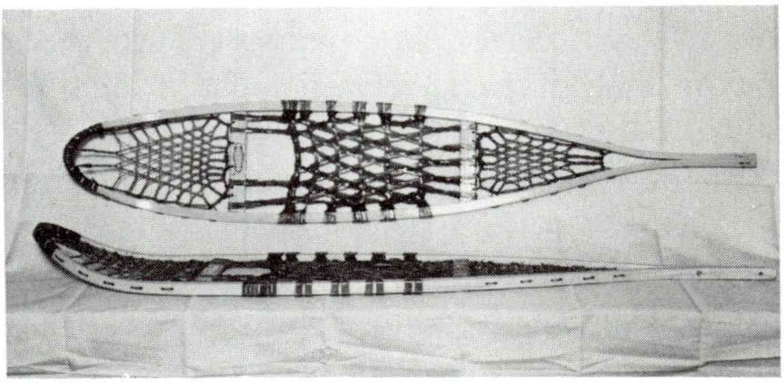

The narrower pickerel snowshoe is for trail travel and long-distance walking in fairly clear going. *Photo courtesy of L.L. Bean, Inc.*

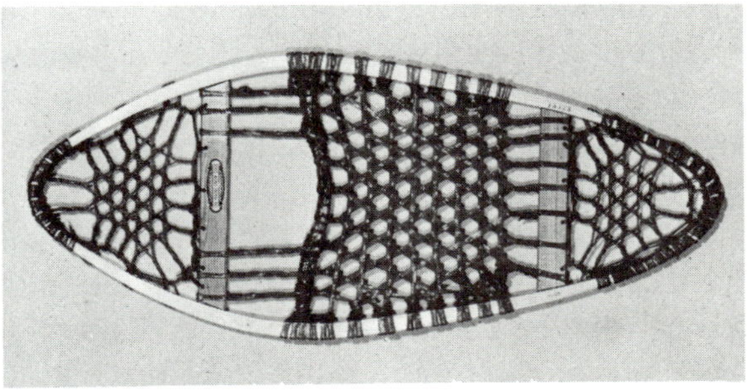

The bearpaw snowshoe is excellent for maneuvering in brushy areas. *Photo courtesy of L.L. Bean, Inc.*

bersome and unwieldy. Despite this drawback, they're popular among icefishermen since a good deal of the travel to a remote lake is done on trails. Standard size of this shoe is 10 inches × 56 inches. It's fine for beginners because its narrow tread and high upturn eliminates interference and tripping.

The Bear Paw Snowshoe is built especially for brushy situations, and is ideal for woodsworkers and trappers, who must be able to maneuver in thickets and densely vegetated areas. The size of 13 inches × 33 inches allows plenty of movement, but isn't recommended for lengthy journeys.

Icefishermen can transport their heavy equipment by carrying a Duluth Pack, also known as a pack basket; a backpack; or a rucksack. Any of these packs will accommodate all the gear required for icefishing, with the exception of an ice-cutting tool. This last item should be as light as possible and should be able to be broken down into two sections for easier packing. I like the spoon-type augers best for this kind of travel because most of them have the two aforementioned qualities.

If a backpack-type arrangement isn't desirable, the equipment can be transported via a sled or specially built sledge. The conveyance can be pulled by hand, or fastened to a body harness or a simple rope around the waist.

Many snowshoers don't use ski poles when walking, but they're handy when negotiating steep terrain. They're also helpful when a heavy load is being carried on the back, which makes it difficult to maintain the proper balance.

Any type of boot can be worn with snowshoes as long as it's warm, waterproof, and snugly fits in the harness. I use my regular felt-lined boots and never have any problems.

Gaiters are useful when snowshoeing because they keep the snow off the upper boot and lower trouser leg. Snow constantly flies about when walking on snowshoes, and wet trousers are the rule unless they're protected.

Cross-country skis are not terribly popular among ice anglers, but the idea is catching on in many parts of the country. Like snowshoes, skis get the fisherman into the backcountry. But unlike snowshoes, skis require much more practice before they can be used with any degree of confidence.

These skis are shorter and narrower than downhill skis, and can be made of wood, fiberglass, polyethelene, aluminum, and other materials. Obviously, the skis are intended to go uphill as well as down, so there's more to learn than the conventional ski slope operation where all the climbing is taken care of by cars, chair lifts, T-bars, and ropes.

Since cross-country skiing involves skill and preparation, the subject is too lengthy to cover in this book. The best way to become familiar with the sport is to take lessons from a pro, or at least accompany a friend who is very good on skis. It's unwise to try to learn alone with no instruction. My very first attempt resulted in a bad sprain, and I was lucky I didn't break a leg.

The technique of applying proper wax is a science in itself. This process is determined by the temperature and condition of the snow.

It's obvious that cross-country skiing is not as quickly mastered as snowshoeing is. A good deal of practice is required to be able to use the slats before a long trip can be taken. Despite this appraisal, skis do have a place in the angling scene, and many icefishermen discover their attributes each year. If you're a serious fisherman and aren't satisfied with an infrequent half-day outing on a close-by lake, you might investigate cross-country skis. There's one thing for sure —they'll open up a whole new part of the outdoors.

Fishing the Forgotten Pond

Icefishermen are gregarious folks. It's not unusual to see hundreds, or even thousands, of people fishing a large reservoir or impoundment. There's no question that winter anglers always head for the same lakes. Every body of water has a reputation, and icefishermen constantly return to the best producers.

It's curious, though, that winter fishermen shun the small ponds and lakes that they fish during the open-water season. Almost invariably icefishermen drive past their favorite little spots and head for big lakes that draw large numbers of anglers.

Many years ago, I discovered that these little ponds and lakes not only produce plenty of winter fish, but offer several other bonuses as well. One winter, a buddy and I cut a few holes in a small lake that was popular among pickerel fishermen in the spring and summer. We never saw anyone fish the lake through the ice, but we were determined to give it a try. We cut our holes over 4 feet of water and set a half dozen tip-ups in likely areas. Three hours later, we had 9 pickerel flopping on the ice. Most were dandies, averaging about 19 inches.

On another occasion, my pal remarked that there was no reason why a certain little pond shouldn't produce big bluegills. After all, it gave up husky fish in the spring, so why not in the winter? We never tried icefishing it before then, and we never heard of anyone else who had either. My buddy tried the pond one day and struck it rich. When he brought a bucket of giant bluegills over to my house that night, I became an instant believer. After seeing those fish, I agreed to fish the pond with him the next morning.

We walked a half mile to the pond along the narrow trail that we normally followed to hunt squirrels and cottontails in the fall. The snow was only a few inches deep, so we had no trouble getting to the pond. I cut a hole, baited a tear-drop with a mousee, and let it settle to the bottom. A moment later, a slight tap suggested a bite, so I snapped the rod tip up and felt the pleasing weight of a solid fish. I couldn't believe my eyes when the fish flopped up through the hole. It was one of the biggest bluegills I'd ever seen, easily measuring close to 10 inches. My buddy pulled up a twin to mine, and we were on our way to a whole new dimension of icefishing. No longer would we ignore the small ponds that are unfished in the winter. From that point on, we would try every one that promised to yield fish.

As the years passed, I had icefished practically every body of water that I could find within a substantial radius of my home town. When I couldn't locate any more possibilities, I purchased topographic maps and looked for hidden ponds that couldn't be seen from roads. On more than one occasion I donned snowshoes and hiked over snowy woodlands to the little waters that were seldom visited by humans in the winter.

Fishing in quiet ponds adds aesthetic satisfaction to an enjoyable sport. A little lake rimmed by hardwoods is a pretty little spot, and even if the fish aren't biting well the natural surroundings help to soothe jangled nerves. That's part of fishing, too.

One of the bonuses of fishing a small pond is the extra period of time you have to ice fish. Small waters freeze over quicker than larger lakes, and also take longer to thaw. Many big reservoirs seldom freeze until January, while little ponds are ready to go by Thanksgiving.

One day I was driving by a tiny pond and noticed two boys pointing down to the ice. I pulled over and walked out to see what they were looking at. The ice on the pond was crystal clear, and every weed and stone on the bottom was perfectly visible. I walked out to where the boys were and looked in the direction that they were pointing. I was amazed to see an 18-inch pickerel finning slowly next to a sunken log. The boys pointed out another pickerel several yards away. In the next 10 minutes we spotted at least a dozen more. Since the ice was clear, the pickerel were spooky. If we tried to approach, they'd dart away and hide in the weeds. It would have been a waste of time to try fishing under those conditions, so I went on my way. I didn't forget the pond and the pickerel, however.

Two weeks later a layer of snow blanketed the area. I returned to the tiny pond and rigged 5 tip-ups baited with lively golden shiners. The snow made it impossible to see through the ice, so the pickerel

Bob Sandstrom hauls in a fine crappie from a small Eastern pond. He's using a Swedish Pimple tipped with a mousee larva. *Photo courtesy of Robert Demetry.*

and I couldn't see each other. I had barely set the last tip-up when a flag waved from across the pond. I ran over and saw the underwater reel turning slowly as the fish swam off with the bait. The line stopped and remained still for about 30 seconds. When it started moving again I set the hook hard. A moment later I pulled a 16-inch pickerel up through the hole. In the next three hours I caught five more pickerel and missed at least that many more. I'll admit that I felt a bit foolish every time a car passed along the road. Here I was, a grown man, fishing in a pothole that wasn't half an acre. But the pickerel were worth it, so I didn't worry about my social prestige.

I'm convinced that one of the reasons that fish bite well in small, unfished ponds is because they see very few baits and lures in the winter. They aren't subjected to the offerings of other anglers, and they eagerly strike lures because they're a novelty. Not only that, but fish in small ponds don't have the volume and quality of feed that big-water fish have.

A nice thing about fishing in small ponds is the fact that the angler can't lament about not finding fish. In some ponds, 15 or 20 holes might be enough to cover the entire surface.

The holes should be located so the pond can be cross-sectioned. Every representative area should be fished. It's wise to remember that in a pond, little factors can have a profound impact on life under the ice. This is the place to watch for the tiny creek flowing in adjacent to the beaver dam, or the windswept shore where the ice is clear. Winterkill is often extreme in small ponds because small volumes of water logically tend to lose oxygen faster. Surrounding woodlands contribute plenty of leaves which sink to the bottom and cause accumulations of gas. The gas then displaces oxygen. Therefore, any areas that have a fraction more oxygen than others would be likely places to fish.

Movement should be kept to a minimum on small ponds because fish aren't used to disturbances and might be spooked by human noises. To avoid continuous disturbance through the day, I cut all the holes I think I'll need before I start to fish. When all the holes are cut, I begin fishing through the very first one I opened. That way the fish will have had a chance to settle down under it.

I like to use smaller baits and lures when I'm icefishing a pond. Small tear-drops are ideal, and very light lines help to register the delicate bit of shy fish. I try to be as unobtrusive as possible on a little pond. Fish can sense human presence quickly, and seem to shun anything but the most perfectly presented offerings.

Fish may be more concentrated in small ponds than in bigger waters, so they might be difficult to find. When they are located, however, a bonanza is usually the result. This is a good reason to cut holes close enough so every area is sampled. Fish may be bunched up between two holes and may never see a bait or lure.

If I'm familiar with a pond, I concentrate my fishing over its deepest water. If I'm not acquainted with it, I look for landmarks that indicate deep water. A steep bank that slopes sharply into the water usually gives away a deep spot. Vertical banks that are undercut may indicate the whereabouts of the channel that is usually the deepest part of a lake. The area adjacent to dams is almost always a deep spot, as is the water next to a retaining wall or dike.

Shallow waters shouldn't be overlooked if deep areas don't produce. One day, I was fishing for pickerel in a small pond, and decided to look down through the hole in order to check the weeds below. When I peered in, I saw several dozen yellow perch suspended just off the bottom. The water was only six feet deep, and there were other

The late Lou Gizzarelli, to whose memory this book is dedicated, as he unhooked a bluegill he'd caught in a tiny New York pond.

parts of the pond that were twice that depth. I was surprised because yellow perch normally frequent the deepest water they can find. It was a good lesson, and reminded me that fish are unpredictable creatures, regardless of their accepted habits and behavior patterns.

Many small ponds across the northern United States are on private land, so permission is often required to gain access to them. Many landowners allow anglers to enter their property, and are amused when people ask to fish through the ice of their tiny ponds. Icefishermen should be sure to pick up litter, and respect the private land. This means using only downed trees and branches for firewood, closing gates after going through, and otherwise leaving the area just as it was found.

Care and Preparation of Your Fish

Since icefishing occurs during a cold time of the year, it's relatively easy to keep fish from spoiling. The most convenient way, of course, is to flip the fish onto the ice, and keep them there until it's time to go home. This is fine if the weather isn't extremely cold. Precautions should always be taken to keep the fish from freezing.

The best way to do this is to cut a hole in the ice with an ice chisel. Deposit the fish in it as they're caught. By cutting the hole shallow enough and punching through the ice to the water below with the bar, the fish can swim about and remain lively as long as is necessary. Obviously the hole that allows water to enter into the depression should be small enough so the captive fish can't escape.

Another way to keep fish is to wrap them with several layers of newspaper. The paper insulates them from freezing air temperatures and keeps them fresh and moist.

If there's snow on the ice, fish can be covered with generous amounts of clean snow. Snow provides good insulation and will allow the fish to remain firm and cold.

Fish should never be allowed to dry out. This is possible even on the ice if the sun is bright and the wind is blowing.

Ice anglers can catch practically every species of fish that's taken in the summer. There are a few bonuses too; some species are laden with delicious roe during the ice season. Yellow perch are heavy-bellied in the winter, and it's always a treat for the family when I fry up perch roe. To keep the roe as fresh as possible, I slit the belly of the perch and remove the roe sacs. Then I pour some clean snow in a plastic bag and deposit the roe in with more snow. This keeps the roe cold, but prevents it from freezing.

Every angler has his favorite technique for cleaning fish, but I

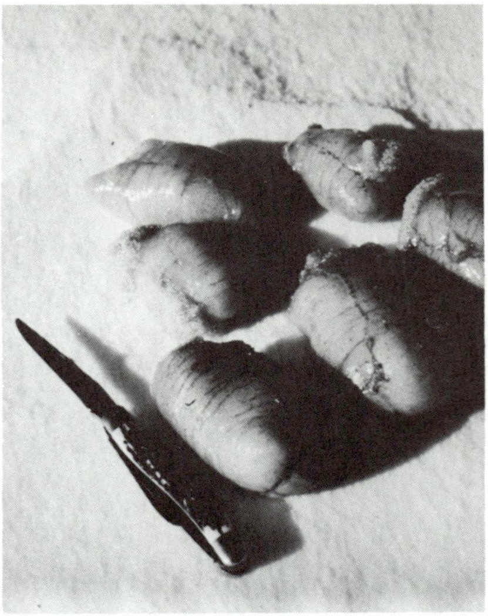

Left: An ice well, cut with a spud bar, keeps fish alive and prevents them from freezing on the ice. To cut a well, chisel a shallow depression adjacent to a fishing hole. Cut a narrow slit from the hole to the well, and allow the well to fill with water. Some anglers prefer to jab a small hole through the bottom of the well, but you must be sure the hole is not big enough for the fish to escape through it.

Right: Perch roe is a gourmet's delight when properly prepared. Mature females are heavily laden with eggs during the winter months. These are typical egg sacs taken from yellow perch in January.

always watch closely when someone is performing this chore. I don't believe that I know all there is to know about cleaning fish, and I'm not afraid to modify my own techniques when someone shows me a better or quicker way.

My old friend, Charlie Booth, taught me a technique to clean bluegills that changed my entire method of cleaning and eating members of the sunfish family. My usual routine was to scale, dress, and behead the fish, and then fry them in one piece. Charlie showed me how to fillet bluegills, and I've never cleaned them any other way since.

The technique merely involves skinning the fish and slicing the fillet from each side. The boneless fillets can be treated like shrimp or lobster when cut into one-inch cubes. I love them boiled, and served with hot butter or cocktail sauce.

Pickerel and northern pike are often claimed to be too bony to eat, but there are ways to make them a delicious meal. They seem to taste

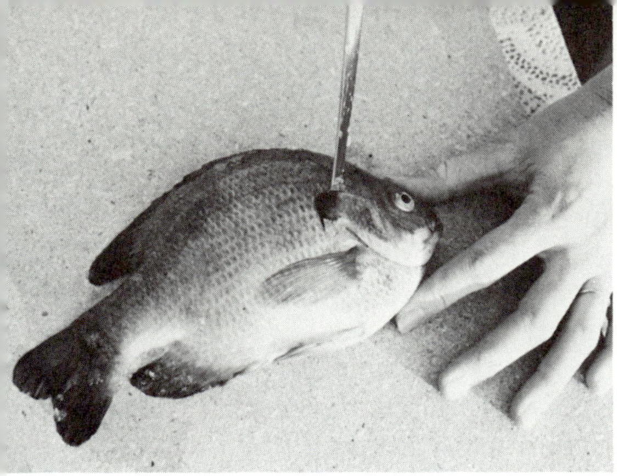

Left: First step in filleting a bluegill is to make a cut from the gill flap to the top of the head. Do this on both sides.

Right: Then, starting at one side of the dorsal fin, slice downward along the backbone to the rib cage. Turn fish over and make same cut on other side.

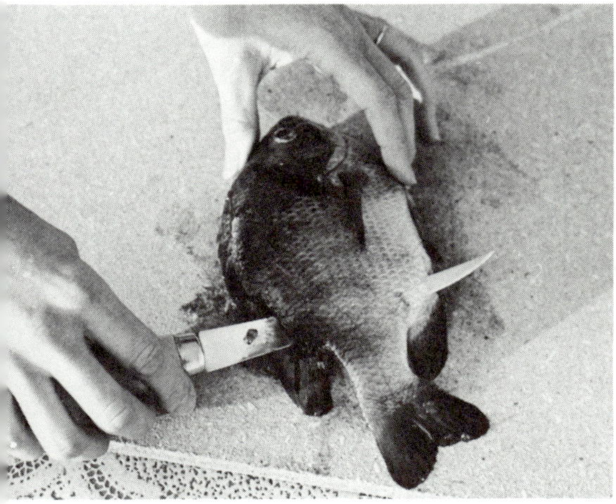

Left: Slide knife in behind rib cage and slice fillet along backbone to tail. Do same on the other side.

Right: Lift fillet and slice it free of rib cage. Continue this cut down as far as there is any meat. Repeat on other side.

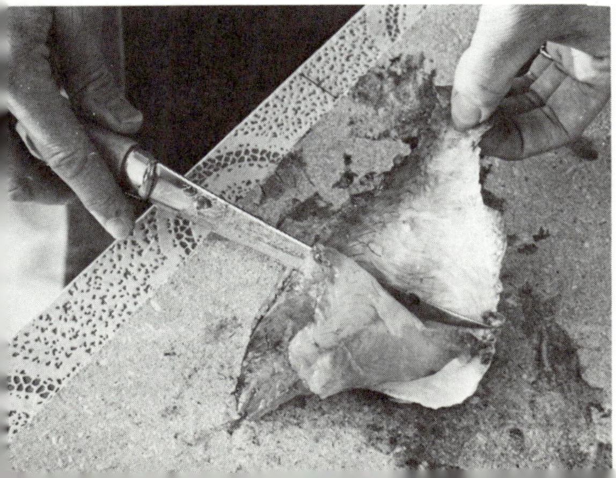

Start at tail, and lay knife flat. Slide it along the skin, and remove flesh. The result is a boneless fillet. Each side makes one fillet.

even better when caught in the winter. The best way to learn how to clean any fish is to watch someone who is skilled at it. There's nothing like first-hand experience, especially since there are little maneuvers made by the knife that might not be described in a series of "how to do it" pictures.

Fish can be cooked all kinds of ways; there are literally hundreds of cookbooks available that detail many piscatorial recipes. Although I like to putter around in the kitchen frequently with a new fish recipe in hand, my favorite serving is smoked fish, especially trout. I'm not alone in this preference, because multitudes of ice anglers across the nation are equally as enthusiastic when it comes to this tasty treat.

At one time the art of smoking was left to a few old-world folks who knew the "secrets," or to packing houses that had the equipment and knew how to turn out a smoked piece of meat.

That's changed now. A dozen years ago, electric smokers were suddenly appearing in backyards, garages, and front porches. The little metal boxes that sent plumes of pungent smoke into the air were on the Christmas list of thousands of sportsmen around the country. Smoked fish were no longer an expensive novelty that could be purchased in delicatessens, but were easily cooked anywhere.

The typical smoker is about 1 foot square and 30 inches tall. It is outfitted with 3 trays to hold the meat, and a hot plate in the bottom. A small pan filled with sawdust or chips rests on the hot plate and smolders, thus producing the required smoke. The sawdust or chips need replacement every 30 to 60 minutes, depending on the kind of material being used. Fine sawdust turns to ash quicker than thick bulky chips. The smokers are normally priced at $25 to $40, and are manufactured by a half-dozen companies.

There are numerous woods that can be used for smoking fish. Some impart a unique flavor to the meat, while others produce a common smoke effect. Softwoods such as pine, fir, hemlock, and spruce should never be used because they're resinous and oily, and will give the fish an undesirable taste. Preferred woods are apple, hickory, hard maple, alder, and most of the hardwoods. My favorite is apple, and I find all I want by visiting orchards and requesting a few chunks of dead wood. Hard maple and hickory give off the same-type smoke, and I've never been able to tell the difference between the two. Sassafras is a species that emits a different odor. I once read an article about an ice angler who smoked his crappies with sassafras wood. I tried it and found it to be delightful.

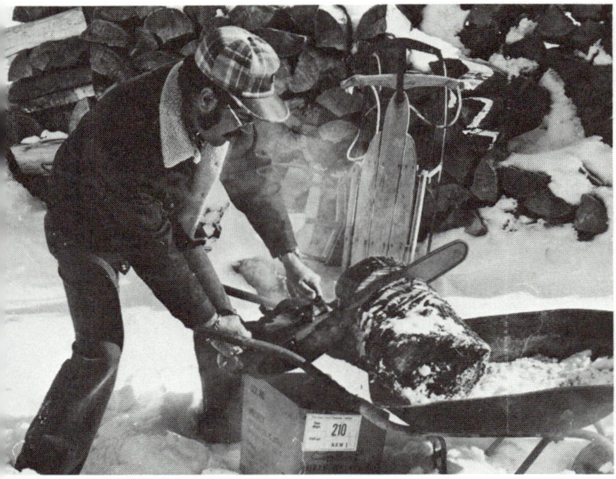

Left: The author makes his own sawdust for the smoker by cutting into an apple log with a chain saw. The cardboard box underneath catches the sawdust.

Right: Ideal way to prepare winter-caught fish is with a small portable smoker. Lois Zumbo, the author's wife, is checking a mess of rainbows. Depending on the size of the fish, six to 20 or so can be smoked at same time.

Sawdust and chips can be purchased in handy containers at most sporting goods stores, but I prefer to make my own. I do it by using a chain saw, a cardboard box, and an apple log. I begin by placing the log across the handles of a wheelbarrow. The cardboard box is located just under the log in the correct position to catch the sawdust. With log and box in place, I begin cutting into the log, angling the saw so that most of the dust flies into the box. I cut about three-fourths of the way through the log, and begin another cut a half-inch away. The wedge of wood left between the cuts is broken off and used to top off the sawdust in the pan. By laying it flat over the sawdust, it smolders slowly and lengthens the period of smoking time.

Someone once asked me if the sawdust was contaiminated with oil from the chain. I've looked the dust over carefully, felt it between my fingers, smelled it, and never found any evidence of oil. The smoked fish never had an oily taste either.

There is no specified time limit when smoking with an electric device. By rotating the trays so that all fish have equal exposure to the heating element, I can have a finished product in 15 to 16 hours. Otherwise the fish can be smoked for 6 to 8 hours and then baked in the oven for a half hour, or until cooked.

Before being smoked, fish must be brined. Salt brine is a preservative that inhibits bacterial contamination. Most bacteria are effectively repelled by a minimum of 5 percent salt. Salt drives out the body fluid and replaces it, adding flavor to the finished product. When the salted fish is subjected to smoke, it becomes firmer and drier.

Most brining recipes state that the brine solution should be concentrated enough to float an egg. I like to be a bit more specific. I add two cups of salt, and one cup of brown sugar to a 1/2-gallon of water. I stir the concoction thoroughly until most of the ingredients go into solution. Then I add the cleaned fish and allow them to soak in the solution according to size. Panfish and trout up to one pound stay for three hours, while bigger fish remain for five to six hours. Small fish can be brined or smoked whole, but bigger ones should be steaked or filleted. I like to cut big trout into steaks, but I prefer filleting walleyes, northerns, and bass.

The addition of salt can be accomplished by the dry technique instead of brining. Simply purchase a quantity of cured salt made especially for smoking. Apply it generously over the inside and outside of the fish. Allow it to stand for 12 to 15 hours before rinsing and smoking.

Some anglers prefer to smoke their fish in old refrigerators, barrels, or elaborate smokehouses. This is a much longer process than the electric smoker, and is generally known as cold smoking. One advantage is that large quantities of meat can be smoked at one time. In the electric smoker, 10 to 20 small fish can be smoked at once. A big 20-pound lake trout will barely fit in an electric smoker, even when steaked. It's obvious, then, that each technique has its advantages and drawbacks.

Pickled fish are popular among ice anglers, especially when large numbers of fish are involved. This is true with smelt, ciscoes, yellow perch, and other species that may be taken home in large quantities. Although there are many recipes for pickled fish, I use a very uncomplicated one. Some excellent pickling recipes deal exclusively with raw, uncooked fish from start to finish. I'm not a trusting soul, so I fry my fish first until thoroughly cooked. Then I cut them in chunks and add them to jars of vinegar that already contain generous slices of onion, parsley flakes, pepper, celery flakes, and oregano. Within a week the fish are pickled and ready to eat. The bones are softened completely and are consumed along with the flesh. I keep the fish refrigerated during the entire process.

Another way to store fish is to can them in jars. My best recipe, called "Spiced Trout," goes like this: Scale trout, dress, behead and remove tails and fins. Cut into chunks. Soak in a salt brine for 1 hour and allow to drain well. Pack the meat in clean jars with 1 slice of onion, 1 or 2 Jalapeno peppers, 1/2 tsp. salt, 2 bay leaves and 1 tsp. of liquid smoke. Place pint jars in a pressure cooker and cook for 1 1/2 hours under 12 pounds pressure (at 5,000 feet above sea level). The fish can be eaten immediately and don't have to be refrigerated when stored.

These three methods are excellent ways to keep fish for long periods of time. Some fish, though, have possession limits, and this rule applies inside the home in many states. In other words, if the law allows a 30 yellow-perch possession per licensed angler, and there are 3 licensed fishermen in the household, then no more than 90 perch can be stored at any one time.

When fish are stored in the freezer, remember that they are perishable and have a short freezer life. Trout in particular, deteriorate rapidly when frozen. Fish should be consumed within a few months after being caught. When being prepared for the freezer, fish should be double wrapped in sturdy butcher paper, and the package should be labeled for easy identification.

I like to store fillets or small fish in plastic, water-filled cartons. The fish are literally frozen in a block of ice and last much longer than otherwise. A friend told me that fish frozen in such a way last indefinitely. I wouldn't know—around my house fish never last long enough to give the technique a long-term test.

When fish are cleaned on the ice, innards should be disposed of properly. Don't drop them down the ice hole, either, especially in a trout lake where there are no scavenger fish to clean them up. In some lakes, crayfish and snapping turtle populations will make quick work of fish remains when spring arrives, but this can't be counted on. Good judgment should be used.

On one particular Eastern lake, five or six crows harassed us constantly when we were icefishing. Knowing they'd clean up the fish remains, we left the offal and heads on the ice after we cleaned the catch. As soon as we reached the shoreline, the crows would happily descend on the ice and clean up every scale and scrap of flesh.

A flock of seagulls did the same thing on a New England lake near the Atlantic Ocean coast. In that case, when we threw fish heads 20 yards away from the fishing area, the gulls landed quickly and fought over them. The birds provided a sideshow and kept us amused when there was a lull in the fishing action.

Unusual Icefishing Methods

There are other ways to put fish on the ice besides the standard hook and line technique. Spears, gaffs, and ganghooks are used frequently, and all require varying degrees of skill. The angler who pursues fish without hook and line actually assumes more of a predatory role, since he doesn't depend on a fish's appetite to capture it. Instead, he must deceive the quarry or at least maneuver it into the right position before it can be successfully ambushed.

Spearing is the most popular of the alternative methods and is practical in a good share of the Northern states. Northern pike, muskellunge, and sturgeon are the chief quarry. Pike are the most sought after of all.

Before continuing any farther in this chapter, let's address the occasional argument that spearing is not a sporting activity. There are some anglers who maintain that if a fish isn't taken on hook and line, it shouldn't be taken at all. According to their viewpoint, spearing takes unfair advantage of the fish. Muskellunge have the biggest fan clubs, and many muskie supporters feel that the fish should never be taken by any means other than open-water techniques.

Spearing enthusiasts feel that the fish are taken fair and square, and that spearing is a highly skilled sport that requires patience and know-how in order to connect with any degree of consistency. Many contend that spearing opponents have never experienced the thrill of merely viewing a fish after waiting long hours in a darkened shanty. They also claim that fish suffer equally as much when they're laying on the ice, regardless of the way they came up through the hole. A fish that is hit solidly with a spear may suffer less from a humane standpoint because it's apt to expire more quickly than one hooked in the mouth by a "straight" fisherman.

It becomes apparent that as long as there is spearing there will be opposition to it. Come to think of it, is there *any* sport that has the blessings of everyone? Certainly not! That being the case, this book will treat spearing as a viable, skillful practice that is a wholesome icefishing activity.

Spearing was prevalent long before white men settled the continent. Eskimos and North American Indians were spearing fish for centuries as a routine winter food-gathering practice.

The modern spearfisherman operates from a shanty. This is not for convenience; it is a necessity. Good visibility is one of the essential ingredients to successful spearing, and only a darkened shanty can provide this requirement.

Here's the standard operating procedure for a day of ice spearing. First off, the spearer cuts a substantial hole inside the shanty—big enough to allow a big fish an easy exit out of the water and onto the ice. In the case of sturgeon, a four by five-foot hole might be necessary. When pike or muskies are the quarry, a rectangular hole two feet by four feet is adequate. An auger shouldn't be used, since the sides and walls should be perfectly straight and squared to allow plenty of clear area for the spear. An ice chisel or spud bar is the usual tool for making a hole with the proper specifications, although chain saws are used in some areas. With the hole cut and every chunk of ice skimmed off, the spear fisherman makes sure that no outside light permeates the shanty. Snow can be piled around the bottom edges to seal them and also prevent chilling breezes from getting in.

Any loose items inside the shanty should be placed away from the spearing area. When a fish is dragged up out of the hole, there are two important things to remember. It will probably be big, and it definitely will be mad. As soon as it hits the ice, it will thrash about wildly, knocking everything around that isn't nailed or fastened to the walls, including the spear wielder himself if he isn't careful.

After tidying up the floor around the hole, the next step is to pull up a low stool, box, or bucket and get seated comfortably. Several hours may pass before a fish shows, especially when muskies or sturgeon are the quarry.

There are a couple different ways to hold the spear while waiting for the fish to show in the clear water. The weapon is heavy, often more than 15 pounds, and is cumbersome and difficult to hold for too long. One of the best ways is to clip the rope that's fastened to the spear to the roof of the shanty so that it will let go instantly upon demand. A more common way is to lean the spear alongside the

A spear fisherman maneuvers his decoy and waits for a sturgeon to appear. This is a technique that requires much patience and skill. *Photo courtesy Michigan Travel Commission.*

shanty wall, but it must be set so it can be eased up into thrusting position without spooking the quarry beneath the ice.

The last step is to lower a decoy into the hole. The decoy can be alive or artificial, depending on the preference of the spear fisherman.

Finally, when a fish approaches the decoy, the spear is either thrust or dropped onto the quarry. With a combination of luck and skill (mostly the latter), the spear will strike the fish squarely in the back just behind the gills. If that's the case, the fish is played cautiously and then eased up to the hole where it's pulled up onto the ice.

Let's elaborate on some details. If a fish detects any movement at all above the ice, it will likely dash away instantly. Spear fishermen must move at only one speed—very slowly. In fact it's best to move not at all.

Some experts keep the spear tines in the water at all times to minimize positioning the weapon after the fish is spotted. Another way to avoid spooking the fish is to wear dark-colored clothing. A white or bright yellow shirt is more apt to alert a fish than drab apparel. A heavy woolen green and black shirt provides plenty of camouflage and is warm besides. Dark gloves are essential, since the hands will be doing most of the moving.

The decoy is an important component of this type of fishing. It must attract the quarry under the waiting spear, and it must hold the fish's attention long enough so the spear wielder can position the weapon properly and let it go. Live decoys are often preferred because they are more realistic. When a big fish approaches, the decoy practically turns inside out trying to escape. It swims frantically about, and sends out delicious vibrations and scents through the water telling the predator that it's chow time.

The big fish is usually turned on by these antics, and may launch a broadside attack on the luckless fish. More often, however, it will circle slowly, as if deciding whether or not this particular morsel is worth the effort. All this time, the spearfisherman is maneuvering the decoy across the hole, hoping that the quarry will follow and present a target right where he wants it.

A live decoy may present problems if it swims upward and under the ice where it can't be seen. The predator fish may nail it with no chance of a shot with the spear.

Artificial decoys are either wood or plastic and must be jigged to offer some realism, especially when a fish comes in for a close look. The jigging must be done with great care so the moving hand doesn't spook the fish. Artificial decoys can be purchased in stores where spearing is popular. Many veterans carve their own.

Live decoys are usually suckers, but big shiners are used when they're available. The decoy fish are either hooked carefully through the flesh above the backbone, or are rigged in a harness that allows them to swim freely.

In some shallow lakes with muddy bottoms, the spear rope is measured and fastened to the ceiling so the weapon will be caught up short just before it reaches the bottom. Thus the water won't be muddied in the event of a miss.

One phenomena associated with underwater objects, when viewed from above the surface, is called refraction. It does two things to the fish below. It makes them look smaller, and makes them appear to be a bit higher than where they really are. By throwing the spear a bit lower than the fish, the refraction error is compensated for. Refraction becomes progressively worse as the object gets deeper in the water.

In some lakes the water may be a bit murky or the spearing location might be over fairly deep water. Since it's usually essential to see the bottom, it becomes helpful to lighten it with corn, oatmeal, eggshells, or beans. A liberal sprinkling of these items will help to outline a fish as it moves close to the bottom.

Spears can be purchased in sporting goods stores, but most are custom-made. Like the spud bars I mentioned in a previous chapter, spears may be handed down from one generation to another. Spears come in different sizes and materials. The number of tines varies from three to ten. Handles can be wooden or metal, depending on personal preference. The rope can be attached to the spear at the head or the very end of the handle. Some spear fishermen claim that a rope joining the head section affects accuracy, but it helps when icing fish. Most important, the tines must be extremely sharp. The points should be quickly honed every time the weapon is loosed at a fish, regardless of whether it's a hit or a miss.

Every spearing enthusiast should be aware of his state's spearing laws. In many states, only certain species may be speared, and there may be size limits on various fish. Judgment is an important part of spearing. The fish that glares at the decoy must not only be correctly identified, but its size must be estimated accurately. Like a bullet, the spear is beyond recall when it's sent on its way. A muskie mistaken for a northern in a state where muskies are protected will be a victim of carelessness and ignorance. An 18-inch northern that's speared in a state where the minimum length is 20 inches will probably be

Left: This beautiful muskellunge was taken by a proud Michigan spear fisherman. Muskies are trophies and are tough to come by whatever technique is used. *Photo courtesy of Michigan Travel Commission.*

Right: A Michigan spear fisherman looks with pride at a dandy northern pike. Northerns are the most sought-after fish by spear fishermen. *Photo courtesy of Michigan Travel Commission.*

These two Wisconsin spear fishermen pose with a beautiful sturgeon. A prize like this will be remembered for years to come. *Photo courtesy of Wisconsin Dept. of Natural Resources.*

These men are hooking carp in an Eastern river. The carp are driven toward the hooks (which point upward and are attached to poles) by beaters who pound on the ice with clubs. As the fleeing carp swim past, the hookers try to nab them with an upswing of the pole. *Photo courtesy of Jerry Gibbs.*

released to die of deep wounds. Few fish survive when hit with a spear, although some that receive only glancing blows might make it. As in hunting, the spear fisherman must be sure of his target.

There is a unique way of taking fish under the ice with special weapons designed for gaffing rough fish, especially carp. The system involves a large group of people, with some of them deployed as "beaters" and the rest as "hookers."

According to Jerry Gibbs, a well-known fishing writer, the beaters bang on the ice with clubs and move in the direction of the hookers, who are bent over the ice looking down into the water.

The alarmed fish are eventually driven under the hookers, who jiggle their elbows just enough to send the hook points swinging directly beneath the fish. When a fish is hooked, it's lifted upward in a swift, smooth motion. Don't stop at the hole or the fish will flip free. It's up and out.

Most of the fish taken are carp, although the technique should work for suckers as well. Medium-sized, slow-moving rivers in the Northeast are selected for this type of fishing. One, in particular, flows by Pine Island, New York, and a group of farmers descend upon it each winter to hook carp. The hooks are homemade, and resemble a double-gaff hook on a long-handled pole.

In parts of the West, kokanee salmon are snagged by ice anglers. Kokanees live only 4 to 5 years and die after spawning. Colorado has a fair number of kokanee lakes scattered around the state. A standard technique is to use a 4/0 treble hook that has a weight attached to the shaft. Ready-made hooks can be purchased in stores where kokanee snagging is popular. For better visibility, the treble can be painted a fluorescent orange or red. The method requires the fisherman to cut a hole over the spawning area, which is usually 4 to 10 feet deep. The treble is dropped into the hole and allowed to lay on the bottom. When a kokanee swims over the hook, the treble is jerked upward. Several kokanee can be taken from a single hole if it's positioned over an active spawning site. Obviously, the trick is to see the fish clearly before yanking the hook. Thus the angler must have good visibility. To accomplish this, the snagger must lie down on the ice, cover his head with a blanket or jacket, and wait patiently until the fish swim by.

In order to stay comfortable on the cold ice, some anglers use a big piece of cardboard or a sheet of plastic to lay on. A piece of foam rubber that's used as a mattress for backpacking expeditions is light, and can be rolled into a small bundle.

The idea of catching spawning kokanees may repel some anglers. Actually, reproduction seldom occurs because the conditions aren't correct for egg survival. Thus, fishermen are merely harvesting fish that would die naturally within a few weeks.

Fun for the Family

Ice and snow offer all kinds of recreational activities. Although icefishing appeals to young, old, and both sexes, there's ample opportunity for the family to find something to do if the fish aren't biting.

Safety should always be stressed; youngsters should be instructed at the outset where the off-limits areas are. Warn them to stay away from inlet areas, open leads, thin spots, and other unsafe spots. It's a good idea to take some time and inspect the locale, making certain that there aren't any hidden spots that might be dangerous.

The most obvious family activity on a frozen lake is ice skating. This is a sport everyone can participate in. Ice skates are also helpful in speeding to a waving tip-up flag that might be half way across the lake. On more than one occasion I've tended five scattered tip-ups by means of skates.

A frozen lake covered with several inches of snow is impossible to skate on, so a snow shovel becomes a necessity to clear a good wide spot. This is one time the youngsters won't balk at using a shovel. When the ice is thick enough, a plow mounted on a vehicle is a quick way to clean off a big area. As a reward, the vehicle operator will gain hero status among everyone who likes to skate.

Sleds and toboggans are great fun when the fishing lake is surrounded by hills. Of course, the usual safety precautions should be followed, particularly if there are enough trees to create an obstacle course.

Energy is consumed rapidly on ice, and in no time young stomachs will be yearning for food. A shoreside lunch is just the ticket; it breaks up the monotony if fishing is slow. My family has settled on a standard menu for our icefishing outings. It includes hot dogs, buns, chili, soft drinks, potato chips, and hot coffee. All the ingredients can be cooked and served without utensils (except for a coffee pot), and paper plates can be burned in the fire afterward. The best way to cook the hot dogs is to skewer them on a green stick. Keep away from cherry, which imparts a bitter taste to food. Also, poison sumac or poison oak may cause serious irritations afterward. We cook the chili by opening a large can of it and setting it in the midst of hot coals. Cooking time is 5 to 10 minutes and requires only warming and stirring, since the ingredients are already precooked.

Brewing fresh coffee over a campfire is considered an art. Only the brave of heart attempt this complex operation. Neither the coffee, nor the water, must be measured. The proper amounts should be estimated in a way that leaves the participants spellbound when the resulting hot liquid is sampled. This type of brew is most commonly called sheepherders' coffee. It undoubtedly gets its name from the folk who began putting it together.

To make it, pour an unknown quantity of coffee grounds into a kettle holding an unknown amount of cold water. The kettle is placed over hot coals where it must come to a boil. As soon as the

Cookouts along the shore are fun for everyone and add enjoyment to an icefishing outing.

liquid boils enthusiastically, it is removed from the heat and set on the ground, whereby a half cup or so of cold water is poured in to settle the grounds. At this point, the coffee is ready to be served, albeit with care, since some of the grounds will invariably refuse to settle in the kettle.

Once the family members are fed, they can go back to their favorite activities. For variation, youngsters always enjoy some type of scavenger hunt. When woodlands ring the lake, the sky is the limit for the little treasures that can be collected by hard-searching kids. The game is easily set up by handing out an identical list to each child. The youngster who brings back the most items on the list over a given period of time is the winner. Some of the items on the list can include bird feathers, pine cones, maple leaves, acorns, etc.

Construction of snow forts and igloos is a fun activity, and will keep children busy most of the day. Mom will enjoy getting involved in this project, too. The only requirement is wet snow that packs together well, or thick-crusted snow that can be handled without crumbling.

If a shallow stream feeds the lake and isn't frozen over, the kids can be employed to turn over rocks and investigate the creatures that live under them. They can gather bait while they're at it, too! Don't forget—if youngsters get wet, make sure that they dry off as soon as possible.

The family dog will enjoy an outing on the ice as much as the kids, but take a few precautions to ensure a happy day. Keep the animal close by or leashed at all times. There's nothing more pesky than a dog that runs across tip-ups, carries off fish, or eats bait. Be extra cautious if there's open water nearby. Fido might run over for a drink and end up a casualty if he can't climb back on the ice.

One of the most popular winter activities in the North is the ice derby or icefishing contest. These are great occasions for family get-togethers, and are often the highlight of the entire season. In many communities, the entire town heads for the nearby lake. In many events, mayors are elected to provide some sort of leadership. Judges are selected to rate the ice sculptures, fish, and young ladies who vie for the queen's crown. These festivals are fun events; even the luckless ice angler has a good time. Most of these events are sponsored by civic clubs and Chambers of Commerce. Everyone is welcome to participate, and Chambers of Commerce are always delighted to welcome newcomers and provide information.

There are a few rules of common sense that apply to family fishing.

These anglers participate in an icefishing contest sponsored by a local organization. *Photo courtesy of Michigan Travel Commission.*

This aerial view shows Tip-up Town in Michigan, one of the largest winter gatherings in the U.S. *Photo courtesy of Houghton Lakes Chamber of Commerce.*

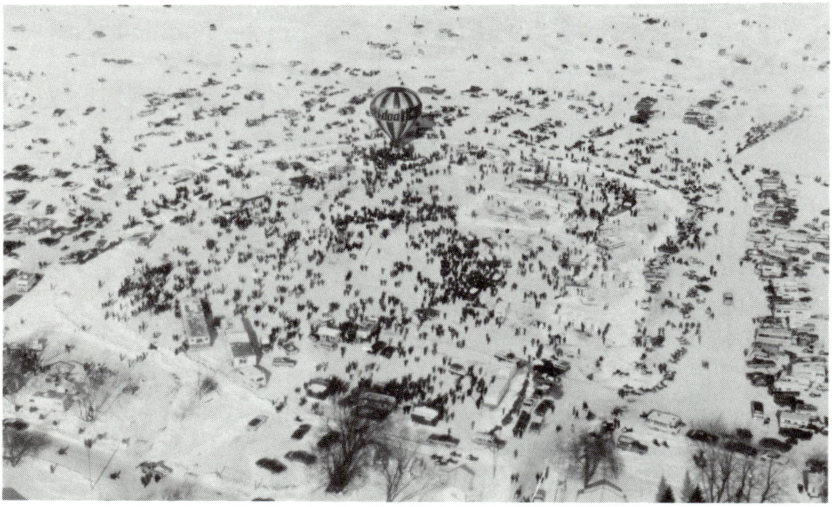

It must be recognized that the attention span of a child is much less than an adult's. Youngsters can't be expected to wait around an ice hole when no bites are forthcoming. On the other hand, when action is hot and furious, kids become glued to the fishing rods or tip-ups and refuse to leave, even though they might be preempting the best holes from dad or grandpa.

Some youngsters have more patience than others. My little girl, Judi, amazes me with her ability to remain loyal to an ice hole, whether fish are coming through it or not.

I started Judi icefishing at age three. During those days, my older children Danny and Janette would pull Judi across the ice on her sled, and park her near a hole where I'd been catching fish. I helped things along by hooking a fish and handing the rod innocently to Judi. When she felt the tug, she'd squeal with delight and run away from the hole with rod in hand. At that point I'd help her clutch her little fingers on the reel handle and assist her in reeling the fish through the hole. After a few fish she caught on and soon began pulling them in by herself.

Because I praised Judi whenever she caught a fish she soon portrayed herself as a good little angler. As the years passed, she took pride in being able to take her share of fish, and insisted on performing chores without help from others.

When I cut a hole, for example, she scooped out the ice chunks by herself. She refused to allow anyone to bait her hook, and she seldom asked someone to take a fish off the hook. One day, when she was six, she sat over a hole for 35 minutes until a trout finally took her bait. It was a great victory when she pulled up a 16-inch rainbow, and I was secretly impressed that she could sit with such rapt attention over a fishless hole.

Janette and Danny enjoy icefishing as much as Judi, and there's always a big contest on to see who catches the most fish. On more occasions than one, dear old dad has finished last.

My wife, Lois, never really enjoyed icefishing until the children were old enough to take care of themselves. When they were babies, there was always a youngster that was cold, hungry, or had to use

This young ice angler is intent on pinning a crappie to the stringer.

the bathroom. Consequently, Lois was a full-time babysitter and couldn't pay attention to fishing, even though I offered my services (only when the fish weren't biting, however).

Youngsters aren't patient enough to try jigging unless the action is consistent. I've found that they much prefer to watch a bobber, especially where panfish keep it dancing. There's a certain mystique to a bouncing bobber, and I find myself using them whenever possible, too. Perhaps the bobber reminds me of my childhood days when I used them exclusively.

Tip-ups are lots of fun for youngsters when the flags are frequently flying. There's always a race, of course, to see who gets to the waving flag first, since the winner gets to try for the fish. Most of the time, one of the kids will always be consistently faster than the others. This results in excessive shouting, screaming, crying, and eventually fighting. The solution is to make them take turns at the tip-up.

When we're using live minnows for bait, I insist on hooking them on myself. Youngsters are usually hesitant about hurting a lively bait fish, and make a big production out of getting a hook through it. This results in the minnow being dropped on the ice many more times than is necessary, and by the time it's firmly impaled it may be dead.

Restrict young children from handling spiny-rayed fish such as perch, crappies, and bluegills. The sharp spines and gill plates can injure a child who grabs the lively fish the wrong way. When most panfish lay on the ice, they flex their fins and spines and flip around wildly. Innocent youngsters can inadvertently receive painful punctures if they try to touch the aroused fish.

Walleyes, northerns, muskies, and pickerel should be avoided by children because of their tooth-studded jaws. A little finger or hand that gets in the way of these teeth might bear scars permanently.

Senior citizens are an important part of the icefishing scene. I know a number of folks in their golden years who love to icefish, and I especially enjoy watching a young lady of 87 who fishes every Saturday with her son. She hauls a lawn chair on the ice, wears a bonnet for sun protection, and has a delightful time while she hauls in a respectable share of rainbow trout.

My mother-in-law never caught a fish in her life until she was 76. One day, I took her, my father-in-law, wife, and children to a little lake brimming with rainbows. She had barely lowered her bait in the water when a trout grabbed it. She squealed with delight and hauled the fish up through the hole. I unhooked the fish, rebaited the hook, and plopped it back into the hole. Within 10 seconds she struggled

This angler, an 84-year-old great-grandmother, relaxes between bites on a balmy Utah afternoon.

with another trout. That action kept up until she had a legal limit on the ice. My father-in-law, who stood beside her, had fared equally as well. A big family fish fry was held the next day.

Patience is very important when icefishing with youngsters and newcomers. Don't expect them to unhook a fish as quickly as you, and don't figure on them catching as many fish as a veteran. Practice makes perfect, and a bit of cooperation and understanding goes a long way in building enthusiasm for the sport.

DeMarr Dudley, 77-year-old father-in-law of the author, proves that senior citizens enjoy catching fish through the ice. Lois Zumbo keeps an eye on the bobber. This small Western lake yields good catches of pan-size rainbows.

Winter Fishing Without Ice

Every other chapter in this book relates to icefishing in the usual straight up-and-down manner. There are times and places, however, where winter fish can be caught in the North without standing over them on a frozen lake. An obvious place is an open stream where water flows unhindered by ice year round. There are others as well.

Some of my fondest memories in New York's Adirondacks were the fishing trips I took to a little flowage that never froze completely over. A strong current kept part of the surface open, and luckily it was on the side of the shore where access was available. The only technique that caught fish was to cast a bait onto the ice across 30 feet of open water. The bait was slowly reeled across the ice, and then was allowed to drop over the edge and into the water. Unless the offering was presented in this manner, the rainbow trout wouldn't strike. I suspect they used the covering of ice for shelter, which shaded them from above. In addition to that specific technique, the trout wouldn't cooperate unless a fresh, whole garden worm was used for bait. Anything less was certain to be rejected.

Since those outings I've had occasion to fish other trout waters that were partially iced over. The same technique worked best on those, too, although other baits were taken as well as worms.

On one memorable fishing trip, I had the chance to try a crazy idea. It was a warm, late-winter day, and huge ice floes were being blown about by the wind. When a big floe came by, I cast my spinner onto it, opened my bail, and allowed the lure to be carried off by the ice. It so happened that the wind was blowing the floe out toward the middle of the lake. Presently my spinning reel was almost stripped of all its line, so I closed the bail and slipped the hitchhiking spinner off the floe, which was then about 175 yards offshore. I had barely turned the handle when I received a jolting strike. About 10 minutes later I beached a 4 1/2-pound brown trout.

If boats were allowed in that lake I would have been in one. As it was, the floe gave me a rare opportunity to fish an area that no one else could reach from shore. That incident points out that brown trout, as well as many other trouts, are much more vulnerable to open-water fishing in winter than in the summer.

I'm fortunate to live just 39 miles from Flaming Gorge Reservoir, which is known throughout America for being the number-one consistent producer of huge brown trout. Many 25-pound trout have come from its waters, including the current world record 33 pound, 10 ounce brown.

Trolling is the most effective means of taking Flaming Gorge's big trout. If you think standing over a hole on a frozen lake is cold business, try trolling on a bitter, windy January day and compare the two. There's hardly a way to excercise while trolling, no fire to stand close to, and no shanty to offer protection from the elements. It's a miserable proposition if the weather is bad, but the payoff can be worth it when a lunker grabs the lure.

An angler must be warm and comfortable in order to be a successful troller. Why fish that little cove across the lake if it's a cold ordeal? All the extremities need extra protection to withstand the rigors of sitting in a cold boat, especially if the craft is working into the wind and there's no opportunity to turn the body away from it.

Cold-weather trolling is productive in many other places in North America besides Flaming Gorge. This is particularly true in temperate states, where unseasonably cold temperatures are usually not cold enough and long enough to form solid ice. When ice starts melting in the North, many lakes and rivers are at their prime for walleyes. When this happens, anglers will dutifully trade their shanties for boats and troll where the action is.

Any type of stream fishing in the winter requires a different strategy than during warmer periods. Fish are nearly always close to bottom, and seldom rise to feed. Worms and live larvae are the most effective baits this time of year. Artificial nymphs and wet flies can work well if bounced along the bottom. One of the secrets in this type of fishing is to use just enough weight to allow the bait to move with the current since it must be kept rolling along the stream bed. The depth of the stream and velocity of the current determines the correct weight, and it may be necessary to use the trial-and-error system to find the right one.

There are two times of the year that cold-water stream fishing is highly productive. In late fall brown trout move up streams to perform their spawning rituals. Rainbows do the same in early spring. In the Great Lakes region, steelhead are often most active when the weather is horrible. The same holds true for salmon runs. Catherine Creek in New York's Finger Lake Region takes on a carnival atmosphere as thousands of fishermen flock to the small stream, hoping to tie into a big rainbow. Many are unprepared for the cold weather, and quit fishing prematurely.

There's one type of stream fishing that's a natural for winter. Mountain whitefish frequent hundreds of streams in the West, and are highly active when the waters are running clear and cold. Whitefish compete heavily with trout for food, so fisheries biologists are eager to see them removed from the stream. Liberal seasons and bag limits are common for whitefish wherever they're found. The best technique for whitefish is to bounce a live larvae or fly on the bottom. These fish school in big bunches, so it's possible to stand in one spot and take several dozen without moving. Since whitefish have a small mouth, a No. 12 or No. 14 hook is about right. Hook the larvae through the collar and pinch a split shot about 18 inches above it. For superb action, use a fly rod or ultra-light spinning rod. Whitefish offer an excellent account of themselves when hooked on light tackle. Although the fish are tasty when cooked routinely, they're great when smoked.

The best place to find them is in long, deep runs and pools. If in doubt, ask locals who live near whitefish streams. Most will be glad to tell you where the best holes are. One word of advice—wear thermal or insulated longjohns under heavy trousers when wading whitefish streams. The water will be coming off of the snowpack in the high country and will be exceedingly cold.

Another form of cold-weather fishing occurs when smelt make their annual spawning runs in early spring. This often becomes a gala event as word spreads that the smelt are running. The standard technique is to dip the tiny fish with long-handled nets. When the smelt are coming on strong, several dozen can be dipped in one scoop. Liberal limits are set in most states, and some measure the take by quarts rather than the number of fish. This kind of fishing lends itself to family fun. A big cheery bonfire keeps the fingers and toes warm during the slow periods. Some folks even bring a skillet and fry up a few smelt on the site.

There's one form of winter fishing that few people even know about. It involves angling for trout beneath the ice of a running stream. I love to try this technique whenever I can. Remember, though, that the ice that covers running water is never safe. That being the case, the best way to approach a likely area is to jump across rocks and boulders. I'm referring to small brooks and creeks, and *not* brawling rivers.

One major necessity is a number of natural openings scattered about in which to present the bait. If a hole is chopped in the ice layer, the trout will spook wildly. In most streams, plenty of spots aren't frozen over, particularly at the heads of pools where mini-waterfalls keep a small area open.

After selecting an opening, proceed with caution so the trout below aren't disturbed. Lower the rod tip down to the hole, flip open the bail, and let the current carry the bait downstream. Sometimes in very shallow brooks I set the rod aside and maneuver the bait by hand. A sharp series of taps and tugs will signal a hit.

Larvae from the stream itself make the best bait. Turn over rocks and pluck whatever you find crawling about underneath them. Brookies are my usual quarry, but any of the trout species can be caught this way. Make sure you check the laws of your state to be sure the streams are open to winter fishing before trying this technique.

Some of the best open-water winter fishing anywhere is found below big dams, in the warm tailrace water. Superb catches of saugers, walleyes, catfish, bass, and most warm-water species are made below dams. The unusually warm temperature of the water keeps fish active and feeding all winter. Bank fishing is effective, although many anglers prefer to do their fishing from boats. Caution is always necessary in the vicinity of tailraces because the water level can rise several feet in a matter of minutes. Hydroelectric demands cause changes of water flow, but most increases in water are signalled in advance by a siren or whistle blast.

Index